# New
# Dayl

CW00485605

**Edited by Naomi Starkey**　　　　September–December 2013

New Daylight © BRF 2013

**The Bible Reading Fellowship**
15 The Chambers, Vineyard, Abingdon OX14 3FE
Tel: 01865 319700; Fax: 01865 319701
E-mail: enquiries@brf.org.uk; Website: www.brf.org.uk

ISBN 978 1 84101 766 2

Distributed in Australia by Mediacom Education Inc., PO Box 610, Unley, SA 5061.
Tel: 1800 811 311; Fax: 08 8297 8719;
E-mail: admin@mediacom.org.au
Available also from all good Christian bookshops in Australia.
For individual and group subscriptions in Australia:
Mrs Rosemary Morrall, PO Box W35, Wanniassa, ACT 2903.

Distributed in New Zealand by Scripture Union Wholesale, PO Box 760, Wellington
Tel: 04 385 0421; Fax: 04 384 3990; E-mail: suwholesale@clear.net.nz

Publications distributed to more than 60 countries

**Acknowledgments**

Printed in Singapore by Craft Print International Ltd

# Suggestions for using *New Daylight*

Find a regular time and place, if possible, where you can read and pray undisturbed. Before you begin, take time to be still and perhaps use the BRF prayer. Then read the Bible passage slowly (try reading it aloud if you find it over-familiar), followed by the comment. You can also use *New Daylight* for group study and discussion, if you prefer.

The prayer or point for reflection can be a starting point for your own meditation and prayer. Many people like to keep a journal to record their thoughts about a Bible passage and items for prayer. In *New Daylight* we also note the Sundays and some special festivals from the Church calendar, to keep in step with the Christian year.

## *New Daylight* and the Bible

*New Daylight* contributors use a range of Bible versions, and you will find a list of the versions used opposite, on page 2. You are welcome to use your own preferred version alongside the passage printed in the notes, and this can be particularly helpful if the Bible text has been abridged.

*New Daylight* affirms that the whole of the Bible is God's revelation to us, and we should read, reflect on and learn from every part of both Old and New Testaments. Usually the printed comment presents a straight-forward 'thought for the day', but sometimes it may also raise questions rather than simply providing answers, as we wrestle with some of the more difficult passages of Scripture.

*New Daylight is also available in a deluxe edition (larger format). Check out your local Christian bookshop or contact the BRF office, who can also give more details about a cassette version for the visually impaired. For a Braille edition, contact St John's Guild, 8 St Raphael's Court, Avenue Road, St Albans, AL1 3EH.*

# Writers in this issue

**Andrew Jones** is Archdeacon of Meirionnydd in Bangor Diocese. He has written *Pilgrimage: the journey to remembering our story* for BRF and is now writing *Mary: a Gospel witness to transfiguration and liberation*.

**Ian Adams** is a poet, writer, teacher and artist working with themes of spirituality, culture and community. He is co-director of the StillPoint project (www.thestillpoint.org.uk) and the creator of Morning Bell, a daily way into prayer (twitter.com/pacebene).

**Veronica Zundel** is an Oxford graduate, writer and journalist. She lives with her husband and son in North London, where they belong to the Mennonite Church.

**Heather Fenton** is a priest, an editor and a writer. She is interested in encouraging lay ministry of all kinds, edits *The Reader* magazine and has recently completed a period as editor of BRF's *Quiet Spaces* journal.

**Helen Julian CSF** is an Anglican Franciscan sister, currently serving her community as Minister General. She has written three books for BRF, including *Living the Gospel* and *The Road to Emmaus*.

**Maggi Dawn** is an author and theologian, currently based at Yale University, where she is Dean of Marquand Chapel and Associate Professor of Theology and Literature in the Divinity School.

**Stephen Rand** is an activist, writer and speaker who now shares his time between persecuted church charity Open Doors and Fresh Streams, a Baptist church leaders' network. He and his wife live in Oxfordshire.

**Naomi Starkey** is a Commissioning Editor for BRF and edits and writes for *New Daylight* Bible reading notes. She has also written *The Recovery of Love* (BRF, 2012).

**Lakshmi Jeffreys**, an Anglican priest, has served in parish ministry, university chaplaincy and as a mission officer across a diocese. She has recently undertaken church leadership in a village just outside Northampton.

**Michael Mitton** is a freelance writer, speaker and consultant and the Fresh Expressions Adviser for the Derby Diocese. He is also the NSM Priest-in-charge of St Paul's, Derby, and honorary Canon of Derby Cathedral. He is the author of *Travellers of the Heart* (BRF, 2013).

# Naomi Starkey writes...

The cover of this September–December issue of *New Daylight* shows lanterns burning as the daylight starts to fade. This image fits well with the season of the year when nights start to lengthen in some parts of the world and we begin to look forward to celebrating Jesus' coming as the light of the world at Christmas. Since moving to the countryside after nearly 20 years of city life, I have become very aware of night-time darkness—and thus appreciative of not only the beauty of moon and starlight but also the value of street lights!

Light guides us on our way, cheers us, keeps us safe, and can also reveal what is really going on around us. The 17th-century theologian and poet Thomas Traherne celebrated his finding of God in creation, uncovering in the natural world the hidden treasures of heavenly love, grace and blessing that he knew were the sources of true happiness. In October we have some readings from Veronica Zundel which introduce us to Traherne and show how his thinking can illuminate our walk with God today.

As light can help us find our bearings, so remembering is important for similar reasons. We use our memory to be aware of where we are, to plan where we should be going and even to keep a sense of who we are, which is why forgetfulness can be such a troubling part of growing older. Helen Julian uses the theme of remembering as a way into the book of Deuteronomy, Moses' great series of sermons delivered as the Israelites prepared to enter the promised land. Remembering what God had done for them in the past would, all being well, guide them to make right decisions for the future.

While Psalm 119 brings us the comforting assurance that God's 'word is a lamp to [our] feet and a light to [our] path' (v. 105), we may need reminding, from time to time, that we are not alone on that path. I greatly enjoyed contributing a week's reflections for the beginning of December on 'The Good Shepherd', recollecting, as I wrote, how 'Emmanuel'—'God with us'—is so very much a truth for every day of the year, and not just for Christmas.

# The BRF Prayer

*Almighty God,*
*you have taught us that your word is a lamp for our feet*
*and a light for our path. Help us, and all who prayerfully*
*read your word, to deepen our fellowship with you*
*and with each other through your love.*
*And in so doing may we come to know you more fully,*
*love you more truly, and follow more faithfully*
*in the steps of your son Jesus Christ, who lives and reigns*
*with you and the Holy Spirit, one God for evermore.*

*Amen*

# Mary, mother of Jesus

As a millennium treat I went to Rome for the first time. It was an extraordinary experience in many different ways, but I shall never forget my first encounter with the spiritual and cultural richness of St Peter's Basilica. I spent time exploring almost every corner of that international place of pilgrimage and what has remained with me above all is Michelangelo's Pietà.

Michelangelo was only 23 years old when he was commissioned to produce this sculpture in 1498, but, to my mind, he managed to create one of the most astonishing representations of Mary we have. The sculpture shows Jesus lifeless on his mother's lap after being taken down from the cross and it is intended to evoke 'compassion' (*pietà*) in those who view it. Unlike so many other depictions of the mourning Mary—anguished and wailing—this one shows beauty and acceptance. Michelangelo shows us a Mary without a furrow or a wrinkle—for me, a visible representation of Paul's description of the church as being 'in splendour, without a spot or wrinkle or anything of the kind' (Ephesians 5:27).

To present a series of meditations based on Mary brings a number of challenges, not least because exploring Mary means facing some controversies. Since the Reformation, the figure of Mary has been an obvious point of division for Christians. Some will want to ask how it is possible to reconcile scripture with the variety of devotional practices around the person of Mary and certain Marian dogmas. Others will want to point out that the various Christian traditions about Mary are nothing like as far apart as some might think, arguing that scripture bears witness to a pattern of grace and hope in God's working, reflected in and through Mary.

During the next two weeks, we will focus on certain passages that are helpful in exploring both the role of Mary as the mother of Christ and some contemporary challenges for us linked to that role. In the first week, I will concentrate on some of the key moments in Mary's life, while, in the second week, I will take you on a journey to significant places dedicated to Mary and her continued witness to the church's mission and discipleship.

*Andrew Jones*

7

# Mary at the beginning and end

After three days they found [Jesus] in the temple… When his parents saw him they were astonished; and his mother said to him, 'Child, why have you treated us like this? Look, your father and I have been searching for you in great anxiety.' He said to them, 'Why were you searching for me? Did you not know that I must be in my Father's house?'… His mother treasured all these things in her heart. And Jesus increased in wisdom and in years, and in divine and human favour.

Luke begins his Gospel in the temple, when the birth of John the Baptist is foretold (1:11–20), and concludes it by returning to the temple, with the disciples gathering to praise God with great joy (24:52–53). Jesus' response to Mary in our passage today links these two temple experiences with this amazing punchline, in which Luke records the first words of Jesus. No longer do Gabriel or Mary or Zechariah or the other angels or Simeon pronounce who Jesus is; Jesus does it himself as he answers his mother.

What appeals to me about Luke's presentation of Jesus' ministry is its sheer humanity. In her reaction to Jesus' presence in the temple, Mary shows that she is the mother of the Lord, yet just like any other mother. Then, after speaking his astonishing words, Jesus does not perform any great miracle but simply goes home and participates in the everyday life of his family: although the Saviour of the world, he is at the same time just like any other boy. All so normal… or is it? Mary and Joseph never quite understand that their son's relationship with God takes precedence over his relationship with them—could this be the 'sword' spoken of by Simeon (Luke 2:35)?

Whatever the mix of normality and divinity in this passage, Mary continued her journey of faith right through to the end and probably never stopped pondering in her heart the true meaning and destiny of her son.

### Prayer

*Lord, as we begin this journey with Mary, the mother of our Lord, help us to ponder in our own hearts the true meaning and ultimate goal of our relationship with the risen Christ.*

ANDREW JONES

# More than a mother

In the beginning was the Word, and the Word was with God, and the Word was God. He was in the beginning with God. All things came into being through him, and without him not one thing came into being. What has come into being in him was life, and the life was the light of all people. The light shines in the darkness, and the darkness did not overcome it.

The opening of John's Gospel brings us to the heart of our Christian faith. Here John seeks to lay before his readers three absolutes: the pre-existence of Christ and his activity in the whole process of creation; Christ's activity in guiding and illuminating humanity; that the incarnation of Christ enables human beings to reclaim their rightful place in the story of God's creation and redemption.

Whatever the controversies surrounding the various traditions associated with Mary—practices, prayers, images, beliefs—one thing is certain: she has a special role to play in God's story. Mary's motherhood is the linchpin of the doctrine of the incarnation. The early church recognised this from the beginning, when it had to defend first the humanity and then the divinity of Christ against all kinds of heretical thinking. I find it arrogant when people accuse Christians of being the recipients of superstitious mumbo-jumbo from an ignorant, bygone age. Those first Christians were not only preaching a message that had a particular appeal for those who lived on the margins of the Roman empire—women, slaves, the poor and so on—but they were also equipping their minds to make sense of how the story of Christ fulfilled and challenged philosophical claims about the relationship between matter and spirit, humanity and divinity.

Mary's motherhood—and more than simply motherhood—made her the first person to be a new creation in Christ. As a symbol, she allows us to contemplate what we are all invited to become in a world without violence (in every sense of that word) and where love triumphs.

**Prayer**

*Thank you, Lord, for your mother and for the way her example continues to invite us to reflect anew on the awe and wonder of our human story.*

ANDREW JONES

# Renewing a covenant lost

Then God said, 'Let us make humankind in our image, according to our likeness; and let them have dominion over the fish of the sea, and over the birds of the air, and over the cattle, and over all the wild animals of the earth, and over every creeping thing that creeps upon the earth.' So God created humankind in his image, in the image of God he created them; male and female he created them.

One of the most interesting titles used for Mary by early church theologians such as Justin Martyr and Irenaeus (and still in the Catholic Church today) was that of the new Eve. While Eve had been defeated by the serpent, Mary defeats the devil by enabling the Son of God to enter the world as Lord and Saviour. Eve's disobedience in the garden of Eden is counterbalanced by Mary's obedience when she said 'yes' to the angel Gabriel.

Catholic traditions surrounding Mary claim that Eve had been dealt a kind of double death by the serpent—that of sin and bodily corruption. The Catholic doctrine of the immaculate conception states that Mary was exempt from sin and the doctrine of the assumption exempts her from bodily corruption as a result. It is by virtue of this double exemption that Mary is referred to as the new Eve.

What I find fascinating about the contrast between Eve and Mary is that, through Eve, we experience disobedience and crisis and, then, when all seems lost, a new way appears so we need not despair. In the message of an angel to Mary, the disobedience that began with Eve can be transformed. In Mary's 'yes' we find a moment that can change the direction and significance of everything which has gone before, a moment in which eternity and time come together seeking reconciliation. In Mary's response—her 'yes'—all is restored and renewed. In Mary, as the new Eve, a new covenant is formed and, through it, hopelessness is reversed.

## Reflection

*'Eva' in Genesis signifies life and Eve was the mother of all things living. 'Ave' was Gabriel's angelic greeting to Mary ('Ave Maria'), a greeting of both love and rescue. May our 'yes' to the call of Jesus bring us to a life lived in all its fullness.*

ANDREW JONES

# Thanks for the gift of life

Hannah prayed and said, 'My heart exults in the Lord; my strength is exalted in my God. My mouth derides my enemies, because I rejoice in my victory'… And Mary said, 'My soul magnifies the Lord, and my spirit rejoices in God my Saviour… His mercy is for those who fear him from generation to generation.'

The process of deciding which books would make up the New Testament was complex and a number of other documents written at the same time were left out. Several of these now make up what is known as the New Testament Apocrypha. One of those books was the Gospel—or Protoevangelium—of James. This document tells the story of Mary's early life in ways that resonate with the life of Christ in Luke's Gospel. Mary's mother, the apocryphal Anne, is closely modelled on the figure of Hannah from 1 Samuel 1.

Indeed, 1 Samuel opens with a portrayal of Hannah—a classic example of an oppressed woman. Unable to bear children, she is scorned by her rival, the other wife within the household. The overall thrust of the story is clear: Samuel is a gift from God to this oppressed woman and his life is, in turn, given back to God as an offering of thanks. To an oppressed Israel under serious threat from the neighbouring Philistines, the figure of Samuel was deeply significant—hence Hannah's song. She exults in the Lord and rejoices in his salvation; none is as holy, none as protective, none as hopeful as God.

After the annunciation to Mary and during her pregnancy, Luke tells us that she stayed for about three months with Elizabeth (1:56). We can almost feel the excitement between the two of them but also their fear and awe—hence the song of Mary. Like Hannah a thousand years before her, Mary exults in the Lord and rejoices in his salvation. As with Hannah, God is the central figure of her song. Hannah's song was fulfilled in the ministry of Samuel; Mary's song was fulfilled in the ministry of Jesus.

**Prayer**

*Let us pray that we find the strength to sing those same songs and, through our own ministries, fulfil the promises of him who is the risen Lord.*

ANDREW JONES

JUDGES 5:1, 20–21 (NRSV, ABRIDGED)

# Another song of triumph

Then Deborah... sang on that day... 'The stars fought from heaven, from their courses they fought against Sisera. The torrent Kishon swept them away, the onrushing torrent, the torrent Kishon. March on, my soul, with might'.

Another song, another woman, another hymn of triumph. The book of Judges covers the period between the death of Joshua and the rise of Saul. With Joshua's death, the age dominated by Moses comes to an end and, with Saul's rise, the age of David and the kings begins to take shape. This transition occurred at a time of danger and uncertainty, when Israel found herself in a threshold place. Weighty questions were asked: how did the followers of the old ways (Canaanites) react to the innovators of the new ways (Israelites)? How would the Israelites interact with different groups of people? How would the people maintain their relationship with God?

Deborah, a judge and prophetess, plays a significant role in this transition from the old to the new as she was a woman of strength and a powerful leader. As a judge, she would have been concerned with, and responsible for, seeking unity and reconciliation and, as such, her moral authority was inspired by God. When her story opens, she is described as habitually seated under a tree between Bethel and Ramah, north of Jerusalem, where the people came to her (4:5). At this time, the Israelites were suffering great oppression at the hands of the Canaanites. Commanded by God, Deborah comes to the rescue and her song indicates the way in which her call for unity and faithfulness saved the day.

There are notable similarities between the stories of Deborah and Mary: both were women of strength, both said 'yes' to God, both sang a song of triumph, and both sang in geographically close locations. What I find particularly interesting, however, is that both women found themselves doing God's work at moments of transition between the old and the new. We become children of the new age, inaugurated in Christ through Mary's faithfulness.

### Prayer

*Often we find ourselves in threshold places. Lord, help us to cross those thresholds with trust and remain faithful in our journey onwards.*

ANDREW JONES

# Not just another mother

When Jesus saw his mother and the disciple whom he loved standing beside her, he said to his mother, 'Woman, here is your son'. Then he said to the disciple, 'Here is your mother.' And from that hour the disciple took her into his own home.

Earlier in the week we made connections between Mary and Eve and considered some of the reasons for Mary being thought of as the new Eve. Interestingly, Jesus is referred to in the New Testament as the new Adam, the new Moses and the new David. He is never referred to as the new Abraham, however: could that be because Mary is the new Abraham?

Abraham did not resist God's call to leave his father's country to go to a new land (Genesis 12:1–4), just as Mary did not resist God's declaration that she was to bear a child through the power of the Holy Spirit. Abraham's faith foreshadows Mary's 'yes' because, just as we are Abraham's children through faith, so we are children of the new covenant, inaugurated in Christ, through Mary's 'yes'.

At the eleventh hour, God restrained Abraham from sacrificing his son Isaac (Genesis 22:11–12), but God did not hold back from sacrificing Mary's son. So, we could actually read Jesus' command in our passage that Mary should look on John as her son as a request: he is asking his mother to see that the one born of her body has to be sacrificed and lost to her as a son, so that we might live.

I remember, as a theological student, having countless discussions about when the Church was truly born: was it at Bethlehem, in the upper room, on the cross, at the empty tomb or at Pentecost? I think it is here in the words 'Here is your son... Here is your mother.' Mary, the new Eve, becomes for us the firstborn of a new reality, a new family, that only God could create. Jesus commands the beloved disciple not to regard Mary as Jesus' mother, but rather to recognise that Mary is 'your mother'.

### Prayer

*Grant us, Lord, faith like that of Abraham and Mary, so we may live as true children of your new family, fruit of the new covenant.*

ANDREW JONES

13

# A great team-player

'I am the true vine, and my Father is the vine-grower... Just as the branch cannot bear fruit by itself unless it abides in the vine, neither can you unless you abide in me. I am the vine, you are the branches. Those who abide in me and I in them bear much fruit, because apart from me you can do nothing... My Father is glorified by this, that you bear much fruit and become my disciples.'

I have always enjoyed trying to spot the 'catchphrases' scattered throughout the Gospel stories. As in secular storytelling, missing them out means the point of the story is lost.

One such Gospel catchphrase is Jesus' use of 'true' or 'truly', 'truly I tell you'. Jesus' use of 'true' in this passage is used in connection with a symbol—the vine. This proclaims him as the fulfilment or even replacement of all Old Testament realities. In Christ, we discover everything that has been prophesied and promised from the beginning.

Although the image of the vine can have several meanings, its connection with discipleship and being part of a team is what attracts me. As 'branches', we are called on to participate in Christ's ministry. We also see that the challenge of contemporary participation goes further when Jesus develops the vine metaphor and mentions the need to 'bear much fruit'. This clearly implies the essential importance of mission activity on our part.

Of the many things that can be said of Mary, as a disciple she was an exemplary 'team player'. She responded well to Gabriel, consulted with Elizabeth and was sensitive to the needs of Joseph. She was courageous in the face of the matrimonial traditions of the day, patient with her unusual growing child and humble about her key role in the incarnation. Finally, she forgave those who abused her son, was grateful to those who supported Jesus, and was accepting at the foot of the cross.

### Prayer

*As disciples of the risen Christ today, participating together in his mission, we pray for a deepening of our ability to be responsive, consultative, sensitive, courageous, patient, humble, forgiving, grateful and accepting.*

ANDREW JONES

# Birthday celebrations

He shall build a house for me, and I will establish his throne for ever. I will be a father to him, and he shall be a son to me. I will not take my steadfast love from him, as I took it from him who was before you, but I will confirm him in my house and in my kingdom for ever, and his throne shall be established for ever.

The books of Chronicles offer a fascinating insight into the history of Israel, stressing that, despite many disasters, God has remained faithful to his promises and, in response, a temple should be built to provide a place in which to worship God.

In these two verses, the author wants to demonstrate the continuity of David's throne and verify the eternal presence of God. Today the church celebrates Mary's birthday—the feast of her nativity. Just as David and Solomon built a house of worship to God, so we can say that, on this day, God 'built' a shrine for the creator of the universe to enter this world: Mary.

It is on a house dedicated to Mary, Joseph and Jesus—the holy family—that I want to focus here, however. To celebrate my own birthday a few years ago, I visited Barcelona and spent some time at Antoni Gaudí's Sagrada Familia (Holy Family). Since 1874, there has existed a group of people who have devoted their lives to constructing a church dedicated to the holy family and they hope to complete the project by 2030.

Three things struck me about the work. First, its beauty reminded me of the essential dignity of the human person. In the Sagrada Familia, our dignity is brought into that of the holy family. Second, the 18 towers and three massive façades will eventually stand as a witness to Jesus Christ. Third, as a basilica at the centre of a bustling international city, it will symbolise the church's missionary engagement with the world. Dignity, witness and mission are what we as Christians should be about today.

### Reflection

*When Pope John Paul II saw the Sagrada Familia he said, 'We must not be afraid of the future nor of each other. It is no accident that we are here— let's build this world together.'*

ANDREW JONES

# An English experience: Glastonbury

In the sixth month the angel Gabriel was sent by God to a town in Galilee called Nazareth… And he came to her and said, 'Greetings, favoured one! The Lord is with you… And now, you will conceive in your womb and bear a son, and you will name him Jesus.'

Since the beginnings of the Church, people have been drawn to Mary for many different reasons and have visited places associated with her. During the next four days I would like to take you to four of these places that have had a particular impact on me. What I found there was a deep 'changelessness' in the face of an extremely fast-moving world of rampant technology, frightening uncertainties and a depth of complexity I had never experienced before. In my own pastoral ministry I often notice how life's tenderness has been squeezed out of people's daily lives. Since everyone has their own personal experience of suffering, disquiet and grief at some point, the changelessness of the places dedicated to the memory of Mary helps today's pilgrims recognise and make sense of how they themselves have changed as a result of their experiences. They are also missionary places, primarily concerned with proclaiming the good news of the risen Christ.

I found all this in Glastonbury, which is the first Marian shrine that I visited and possibly the oldest and most popular in England. It was in the contrast between Glastonbury's changelessness and my own personal spiritual and emotional ebb and flow that I found healing.

Luke tells us that the angel Gabriel went to a place called Nazareth to meet Mary. Sadly we cannot do that, but we can go to places such as Glastonbury to encounter the gospel values that Mary has passed on to us.

## Prayer

*Lord, teach us to treasure all your words and ponder them in our hearts. We ponder also the words you taught Mary to say and we make them our own. Lord, we glorify you. We rejoice in you, our Saviour. We thank you for the wonders you have worked for us. We praise your name, we trust in your loving mercy. Help us to do whatever you tell us.*

Part of the Glastonbury Prayer

ANDREW JONES

# A Welsh experience: Llŷn Peninsula

By the tender mercy of our God, the dawn from on high will break upon us, to give light to those who sit in darkness and in the shadow of death, to guide our feet into the way of peace.

This verse introduces a theme that runs right through the Gospel of Luke—one that is basic to the whole New Testament—namely that of peace. This peace is not merely the cessation or absence of hostilities. Its focus is on wholeness, harmony, well-being, prosperity and security. Throughout Luke's Gospel, it interconnects with the experience of love, particularly love for those who are different. It is worth noting that the first word of the crucified and risen Jesus to his disciples is 'Peace' (24:36).

It is also no coincidence that modern-day pilgrims, time and again, travel in pursuit of wholeness, harmony, well-being, prosperity and security. This is why a pilgrimage is fundamentally different from a day out or a holiday on the beach. The latter can certainly provide rest and refreshment, but a pilgrimage seeks to achieve more.

I live and work on an ancient pilgrimage route that meanders westwards along the Llŷn Peninsula in north-west Wales. Along the way, pilgrims encounter a string of churches, wells, shrines and ancient stones as they journey to Bardsey Island. Right at the tip of the peninsula and just before crossing a treacherous stretch of water, pilgrims encounter Mary. Even here—a place that was once the most westerly edge of the Roman Empire—Mary has been commemorated for the best part of 1500 years. In a field above the valley down to the sea, there once stood a church dedicated to Mary (its outline can still be seen) and you can climb down steps hewn out of the rock called Grisiau Mair, the 'Stairs of Mary'. At the bottom of the steps there is a well—St Mary's Well—where pilgrims have sought the protection of Mair, Morwyn y Mor, 'Mary, the Virgin of the Sea'. These ancient traditions connect to a time when Mary was, as is still the case in many places in the world, everyone's local saint.

**Prayer**

*Lord, guide our feet into the way of peace.*

ANDREW JONES

17

# A Polish experience: Częstochowa

Therefore the Lord himself will give you a sign. Look, the young woman is with child and shall bear a son, and shall name him Immanuel.

During King Uzziah's reign, the kingdom of Judah reached the peak of its strength. Under Ahaz (Uzziah's grandson), things declined rapidly, but, although Ahaz was a weak leader, he was supported by the prophet Isaiah. King Ahaz needed to make a decision regarding the future prosperity of Judah and some of his advisers said one thing and Isaiah another. Ahaz sought confirmation of Isaiah's words, but, despite the sign spoken of here, his mind was already closed. Although Isaiah could not persuade him, sometime in the future truth would be confirmed. The promised child would guarantee the kingdom's future and, for this reason, he could be called Immanuel because, ultimately, the fulfilment of Isaiah's promise would reveal the closeness and intimacy of God.

Not far from my home is a large Polish community and, over the years, I have befriended many Polish priests and accompanied them to almost every corner of Poland, including Częstochowa, which is linked to one of the most charming of the legends concerning Mary. It tells how, in fulfilment of Jesus' dying words, she went to live with John the beloved disciple, taking with her a table that Jesus had made, on which Luke painted a portrait of Mary. Eventually, the portrait reached Poland and was hung in the monastery of Jasna Góra (the 'Luminous Mountain') in Częstochowa, where it remains to this day and is known as the Black Madonna of Jasna Góra.

Over the years, Poland has suffered greatly and this pilgrimage site has been the focus of prayer in the face of persecution. Just as in the days of Isaiah and Ahaz, Poland has been faced with significant decisions. Unlike Ahaz, the Polish nation—especially thousands of its young people who gather daily at Częstochowa to pray—has remained committed to God.

### Reflection

*Pope John Paul II, during a visit to Częstochowa, said, 'To be a Christian is to be on a constant vigil. As a mother is on vigil by her child, to be on a vigil is to protect the value of good.'*

ANDREW JONES

# A Spanish experience: Montserrat

While [Jesus] was still speaking, suddenly a bright cloud overshadowed them, and from the cloud a voice said, 'This is my Son, the Beloved: with him I am well pleased; listen to him!' When the disciples heard this, they fell to the ground and were overcome by fear. But Jesus came and touched them, saying, 'Get up and do not be afraid.'

Climbing mountains to seek God occurs throughout the Bible. Abraham, Moses, Elijah and David all experienced God's presence on a mountain. Jesus drew crowds up hills and revealed the power of God through his words and actions. Perhaps the most extraordinary mountain-top experience is the transfiguration, recorded in each of the Gospels and lying at the heart of Jesus' earthly ministry.

Like many people, I too have climbed mountains and encountered a glimpse of the eternal, as Peter, James and John did on Mount Tabor when Jesus was transfigured before them. Perhaps my most striking mountain-top experience took place at Montserrat in Spain—a mountain in the foothills of the Pyrenees where, in a monastery, stands a wooden statue of Mary and Jesus called La Moreneta ('dark little one'). Tradition has it that it was carved in Jerusalem when James was leader of the church there, whose own shrine lies on the opposite shore of Spain in Santiago de Compostela. Millions of people visit this place annually and, as I did, describe it as a place of transfiguration.

What does transfiguration mean today? First, it is the strength received in particular places that enables us to see the reflection of God in a new way in other people and the world. Second, it was primarily an experience of worship. The more we get caught up in worshipping generously, the more we will experience the grace of transfiguration—that is, see things more as God sees them. We will realise, as several of the early church writers said, that the glory of God is men and women fully alive.

### Prayer
*Jesus said, 'I came that they may have life, and have it abundantly' (John 10:10). Lord, may the grace of transfiguration help us to live life to the full.*

ANDREW JONES

# Ecumenical opportunities

[Jesus said] 'I ask... that they may all be one. As you, Father, are in me and I am in you, may they also be in us, so that the world may believe that you have sent me. The glory that you have given me I have given them, so that they may be one, as we are one.'

After the last supper, Jesus delivers the most powerful after-dinner speech ever (John 13:21—17:26). He clearly recognises that the end of his earthly life is imminent and wants to underline the essential parts of his ministry. The speech ends with a rallying prayer for unity, which is in two dimensions—vertical and horizontal. The vertical dimension grounds unity in the relationship between Jesus and God and the horizontal is seen in the command to love one another, the expression of that relationship being brought about by members of the community.

Mary is sometimes discussed as if she was simply a divisive topic for Christians, but this is a huge oversimplification. The person of Mary must lie at the heart of the theological issues surrounding ecumenism, for Christ did not simply drop down from heaven; he was born of a woman (Galatians 4:4). The faith of the Church is necessarily anchored in history and Mary stands as a guarantee that the incarnation cannot be a marginal teaching. She is also the guarantee of the reality of human salvation: that God's grace reaches down into the roots of humanity and makes human beings holy before God then and now, not in a future eternity.

Looking at the characters in the Bible, God chose some very unlikely people to bring about his purposes—and he still does. Nowhere is this clearer than in the choice of Mary—a young, inexperienced and unknown girl from Galilee. Most of us would never have chosen the likes of her to launch an important venture, but God did and we can see how effective she was. She had lots of humility and lots of grace, an unbeatable combination.

### Reflection

*It is true that various Christian traditions disagree about Mary's status, but it is a good idea to try and hold on to the basics. God chose her to bring Christ into the world and, to me, that is pretty special.*

ANDREW JONES

# Contemporary challenges

In those days Jesus came from Nazareth of Galilee and was baptised by John in the Jordan. And just as he was coming up out of the water, he saw the heavens torn apart and the Spirit descending like a dove on him. And a voice came from heaven, 'You are my Son, the Beloved; with you I am well pleased.'

Imagine if we had only Mark's Gospel! We would have no annunciation to Mary, no Christmas, no Epiphany, no knowledge that Jesus and John were cousins… but the church's traditions surrounding baptism might have even more significance than they do. Maybe we would each remember the date of our own baptism as a significant milestone, reflecting our entry into the family of faith.

We are not told why Jesus sought John's baptism, but we do know that the baptismal experience revealed his identity. Does our baptism say something about our own Christian identity? The tearing apart of the heavens described in our passage today symbolises the end of separation from God and the beginning of direct communication between heaven and earth. Do we feel in touch with God?

The Spirit descended like a dove and so Jesus' baptism links him to the creation of the world, when the Spirit hovered over the waters. Are we able to connect with the divine roots of where we have come from?

The heavenly voice confirms the existing relationship between God and Jesus. Is it clear to us that we too are related to God through Jesus?

You might be thinking, 'Why end these meditations on Mary with a passage about Jesus' baptism from the Gospel that shows the least interest in Mary?' First, many of us are presented for baptism by our mothers, but this was not so in Jesus' case. It is almost as if Mary had completed her role and, instead of presenting him to John for baptism, she presented him to all of us for eternity. Second, baptism is the beginning of a new adventure, for Jesus and for us. It is a covenant that unites all Christians, regardless of tradition.

### Reflection

*Through baptism we enter into a life of discipleship, witnessing to the splendour of truth, the beauty of holiness and the fruit of the relationship we have with Christ, just as Mary did.*

ANDREW JONES

# Jesus' wisdom in Luke 17—20

Luke is a wonderful storyteller. His stories have colour, life and momentum and surprise us. Everywhere the Jesus of Luke's Gospel goes, either lives are changed for good or people are enraged. We will see this mix in the stories of the blind man healed, the tree-climbing tax collector and various others featuring angry or at least argumentative religious leaders.

We will also encounter a Jesus whom we may find uncomfortable in some ways. This Jesus may not sit easily with what we think we know of him. We will discover that when something destructive needs to be resisted, there can be an abrasive side to him. He is sometimes awkward, demanding, difficult and even troubling. His own stories have a bite to them and he is not afraid, to borrow a Quaker phrase, to 'speak truth to power'. He will get us thinking hard about the challenges within our society generated by issues of shame and blame, deceit and the pursuit of status. We will also ponder the life-changing possibilities of qualities revealed by Jesus, such as mercy, presence and inner transformation. We will learn from the wisdom of children and be inspired by a man who comes back to give thanks when all the others apparently forgot.

The wisdom of Jesus is a gift to the world. Whatever our background, faith or spiritual path, we will find his wisdom to be accessible and insightful. At the time he was teaching, people were apparently astonished by his authority. I sense that this came from a powerful mix of humility (as the 'beloved Son', he really did not need to prove anything to anyone), of authenticity (he clearly lived out what he taught) and of love (he knew and loved the faith tradition from which he emerged).

There is one other vital thing about the wisdom of Jesus: it does not come as teaching alone. Rather, Jesus himself comes to us; he himself is present with us. So, as we encounter his wisdom in these next two weeks of readings, may we find ourselves being drawn towards him—this compassionate and hopeful Jesus, this Jesus alongside whom we may weep, but also in whose presence we may face a turbulent world with a quiet new confidence.

*Ian Adams*

# Ending the shame-and-blame process

Jesus said to his disciples, 'Occasions for stumbling are bound to come, but woe to anyone by whom they come! It would be better for you if a millstone were hung around your neck and you were thrown into the sea than for you to cause one of these little ones to stumble. Be on your guard! If another disciple sins, you must rebuke the offender, and if there is repentance, you must forgive. And if the same person sins against you seven times a day, and turns back to you seven times and says, "I repent", you must forgive.'

Two phrases of Jesus to begin this series on the wisdom of Jesus in Luke's Gospel: 'Be on your guard!' (v. 3) and 'you must forgive!' (v. 4). In these two demanding phrases Jesus recognises the twin problems that beset so many of our attempts to be good human beings—shame and blame.

The roots of our shame—our mistakes, failures and 'occasions for stumbling' (v. 1)—are, says Jesus, bound to happen. This is, in part, just a simple challenge from him to us to be aware of our own potential for actions (or inactions) that may lead to shame growing within us. It is a call to self-awareness regarding our seemingly limitless capacity for messing up, that we need to be on our guard! At the same time, there is a specific reminder here of the absolute necessity for our duty of care regarding the young and vulnerable, lest we 'cause one of these little ones to stumble' (v. 2). In the last few years, we have all become aware of how this duty has so often been abandoned and 'little ones' have been used and abused. Again, we need to hear this call and be on our guard!

Whatever the roots of our own shame, it is so easily transferred to those whose wrongdoing (we may imagine, pretend or believe) is greater than our own. This progression from shame to blame seems to be one of the primary impulses driving contemporary society. The insightful teacher Jesus wants to help us stop this destructive process. His remedy is simple but demanding: 'you must forgive' (v. 4).

### Prayer
*Lord, help me today to forgive.*

IAN ADAMS

# Mercy ripples out

On the way to Jerusalem Jesus was going through the region between Samaria and Galilee. As he entered a village, ten lepers approached him. Keeping their distance, they called out, saying, 'Jesus, Master, have mercy on us!' When he saw them, he said to them, 'Go and show yourselves to the priests.' And as they went, they were made clean. Then one of them, when he saw that he was healed, turned back, praising God with a loud voice.

'Mercy' is an old-fashioned kind of word, but one full of possibility in terms of the sort of change within us that we could make to bring good to the world. The call for mercy is one that flows through the stories surrounding Jesus in Luke 17—20. In the episode described in our passage today, for example, ten people who are suffering from the dreaded disease described as 'leprosy' (though probably not what we know today as leprosy)—cast out, shunned and forgotten by their communities—plead for mercy from Jesus. The compassionate Jesus enables a quiet miracle, telling the lepers to do what is necessary to be readmitted to their community—show themselves to the priests. In their faithful response they experience the mercy they seek.

One of the interesting things about Jesus' take on the idea of mercy is that it always seems to be just the beginning of something new: it must ripple out. For Jesus, mercy cannot be contained, cornered or resisted. His famous Beatitude saying has at its centre mercy rippling out: 'Blessed are the merciful, for they will receive mercy' (Matthew 5:7). The mercy shown to the lepers is a mercy that, Jesus hopes, will produce mercy-filled lives in them. The sad end to the story, though—only one of the ten returning to thank Jesus and give praise to God—is a reminder of the persistence that may be required of us when we embrace lives of mercy. The mercy we offer may not always be passed on, but we are still to heed the call to be people of mercy as we walk the way of Jesus.

## Reflection

*If you can, drop a few pebbles into water today. Let the ripples be a sign of your commitment to mercy.*

IAN ADAMS

# Transformation starts close in

Once Jesus was asked by the Pharisees when the kingdom of God was coming, and he answered, 'The kingdom of God is not coming with things that can be observed; nor will they say, "Look, here it is!" or "There it is!" For, in fact, the kingdom of God is among you.'

This question from the Pharisees to Jesus seems to be a genuine one. It is not an attempt to catch him out, but an example of how the often-maligned Pharisees are, at their best, seeking to walk a genuine path towards love of God and love of neighbour. The enigmatic idea of the coming kingdom of God or heaven is always close to the centre of Jesus' teaching, so the question is real and the answer matters for the Pharisees. Different groups of kingdom-seekers within Judea at that time imagined the kingdom of God in different ways and, therefore, had different views on how and when it might come. Religious purity in the temple, finely observed religious practice in daily life, extreme asceticism in the desert or the violent overthrow of the occupying Romans each had their own advocates.

In our world, which needs to change so much, the question of the coming kingdom is as relevant as ever. So, Jesus' answer to the Pharisees is as important to us as it was to them.

The peaceable kingdom, the state of everything good flourishing, does not begin anywhere 'out there' but must begin within us. We can only help transform the world to the extent that we are transformed ourselves. We cannot grasp for it somewhere outside of our own selves. Rather, in God's care, the peaceable kingdom is already within us waiting to be released: 'the kingdom', says Jesus, 'is among you' (v. 21). This should be cause for joy and hope as, however bad things seem to get (and they do get bad), the hope-full alternative is always close to hand. The kingdom is happening within us and around us. Our call is to open ourselves up to its energy and allow the transformation to take shape in us and around us.

**Prayer**

*Your kingdom come, within me and around me.*

Ian Adams

# Lose to find

[Jesus said to his disciples] 'Remember Lot's wife. Those who try to make their life secure will lose it, but those who lose their life will keep it. I tell you, on that night there will be two in one bed; one will be taken and the other left. There will be two women grinding meal together; one will be taken and the other left.'

Lose in order to keep. Let go to find. Unhand to be held. Welcome to the counter-intuitive wisdom of Jesus.

In this episode from Luke's Gospel, Jesus' teaching for the disciples emerges out of a conversation with the Pharisees about the coming kingdom. Jesus has made it clear that the peaceable kingdom we seek begins within us and it begins now. In the teaching that follows, he speaks of the completion of that process, 'when the Son of Man [a favourite saying that Jesus uses to describe himself] comes' (18:8). Then he offers a key teaching for anyone interested in living in the light of this day of revelation and this peaceable kingdom: 'Those who try to make their life secure will lose it, but those who lose their life will keep it' (17:33).

To give local colour to what he is saying, Jesus refers back to an old story from Jewish scriptures, in which Lot's wife looked back to the security of her former home (Genesis 19:26). He recognises how diffi-cult this call to 'lose life' will be for us, with as many rejecting this stance as there are accepting it.

This teaching feels deeply counter-intuitive—to live a life open to loss rather than focused on gain, open to descent rather than seeking ascent, open to uncertainty rather than trusting only security. This is the demanding path of faith to which we are called—demanding but amazingly freeing, for, in losing your life in this way, you may truly discover it.

## Reflection

*Take time today to reflect on the extent to which you sense you may be living out of a desire for security at this time in your life. Then ask yourself what might change if you ventured towards the kind of 'losing to keep' that Jesus is suggesting?*

IAN ADAMS

# Let go of the comparisons

[Jesus] also told this parable to some who trusted in themselves that they were righteous and regarded others with contempt: 'Two men went up to the temple to pray, one a Pharisee and the other a tax-collector. The Pharisee, standing by himself, was praying thus, "God, I thank you that I am not like other people: thieves, rogues, adulterers, or even like this tax-collector. I fast twice a week; I give a tenth of all my income." But the tax-collector, standing far off, would not even look up to heaven, but was beating his breast and saying, "God, be merciful to me, a sinner!"'

It is something that we do all the time—comparing ourselves to others. It is almost always a damaging process, but there is an alternative.

This is one of Jesus' great parables. It asks us to consider our sense of self-awareness. The two men in the parable exhibit very different levels of understanding in this area. They are both at prayer in the temple. One, the Pharisee, exhibits virtually no self-awareness at all, focusing on how he is not like others (never a good place to begin a process of reflection and self-examination) and on his own perceptions of his apparently blameless life: 'God, I thank you that I am not like other people…' (v. 11). The other man, the tax-collector, looks within his own heart and recognises there the depth of his neediness. All he says is, 'God, be merciful to me, a sinner!' (v 13). Jesus goes on to say that he is the one who goes home 'justified'. The tax-collector senses that he is loved and forgiven, and we can imagine that he will therefore be happy and merciful towards those whom he will encounter.

If we read this parable as exploring the way that we compare ourselves with others, something emerges clearly. The truth is, the more we indulge in such behaviour, the less self-aware we are likely to become. On the other hand, the more self-aware we become, the less interested we will be in this destructive process of comparison.

### Reflection

*Try to observe yourself today. See when and how you compare yourself with others. Let go of the comparisons.*

Ian Adams

# Learning from the children

People were bringing even infants to him that he might touch them; and when the disciples saw it, they sternly ordered them not to do it. But Jesus called for them and said, 'Let the little children come to me, and do not stop them; for it is to such as these that the kingdom of God belongs. Truly I tell you, whoever does not receive the kingdom of God as a little child will never enter it.'

What might it be like to 'receive the kingdom of God as a little child' (v. 17)? The people come to Jesus for his healing and blessing and, Luke tells us, they bring their children for the same purpose. This clearly does not meet with the approval of some of the disciples and they try to stop it. Perhaps it all feels too chaotic or not serious enough or just too noisy, but Jesus is clear that the children must not be stopped and he continues to bless them. There is something both basic and vital here about ensuring that children are always loved, accepted, welcomed and protected.

Jesus also offers some wider lessons to learn here. The peaceable kingdom (which starts here and now, within us and around us) can be seen to be at home with children. It belongs to them, he says, because they receive it in the right way. So, what is their way of engaging with the kingdom? We cannot know for sure what Jesus is suggesting, but it might be something to do with the way that children naturally sense their belonging and connection. They set out in life loved and loving, connected and connecting, knowing their deep at-oneness, and it is only the toughness of life experiences that begin to suggest anything else. The kingdom of God, too, is our true place of belonging and way of being—how could we have imagined anything else? This is perhaps why discovering (or rediscovering) the Christ as adults can feel like a homecoming. This is what we were born for!

### Prayer

*Holy Trinity, thank you that I belong to you and in you. Help me to receive you and your kingdom like a child, loved and loving, connected and connecting, at one.*

IAN ADAMS

# Follow me

A certain ruler asked him, 'Good Teacher, what must I do to inherit eternal life?' Jesus said to him, 'Why do you call me good? No one is good but God alone. You know the commandments: "You shall not commit adultery; You shall not murder; You shall not steal; You shall not bear false witness; Honour your father and mother."' He replied, 'I have kept all these since my youth.' When Jesus heard this, he said to him, 'There is still one thing lacking. Sell all that you own and distribute the money to the poor, and you will have treasure in heaven; then come, follow me.' But when he heard this, he became sad; for he was very rich.

'There is still one thing lacking' (v. 22): these are tough words from Jesus to a man who wishes to follow him. It becomes clear in this story from the life of Jesus that 'the one thing lacking' in the case of this man has something to do with his unhealthy connection to his wealth. Elsewhere in Jesus' teaching he makes it clear that great wealth is a particular challenge to anyone seeking to follow him. It is not that he rules out wealth: we know that he himself is provided for in part by some wealthy women and he seems interested in what we do with wealth if it ever comes our way. The foundational issue here is our attitude towards the things that give us security. Do they free us or do they actually grasp us and keep us prisoner?

Luke is clear that Jesus is compassionate. His Gospel is full of stories of Jesus' love, empathy and mercy, but Luke also shows us a Jesus who (usually quietly but persistently) calls us to follow him. So, as we hear that call to follow him again for ourselves—and that call comes every day if we are alert to it—perhaps an important question is this: what might be 'the one thing lacking' for each one of us? Is there something holding us back from taking Jesus' path today?

### Prayer

*Compassionate Jesus, help me to face today's 'one thing lacking'*
*and, once again, follow you.*

IAN ADAMS

# 'What do you want?'

As [Jesus] approached Jericho, a blind man was sitting by the roadside begging. When he heard a crowd going by, he asked what was happening. They told him, 'Jesus of Nazareth is passing by.' Then he shouted, 'Jesus, Son of David, have mercy on me!' Those who were in front sternly ordered him to be quiet; but he shouted even more loudly, 'Son of David, have mercy on me!' Jesus stood still and ordered the man to be brought to him; and when he came near, he asked him, 'What do you want me to do for you?' He said, 'Lord, let me see again.' Jesus said to him, 'Receive your sight; your faith has saved you.' Immediately he regained his sight and followed him, glorifying God; and all the people, when they saw it, praised God.

What do you want? An answer to that question may come to you at once or it might end up being a little more complicated.

A man who is blind is begging by the side of the road. Hearing the noise of a gathering crowd, he asks what is happening and, having discovered that the (by now well-known) healer-teacher Jesus of Nazareth is heading through town, he cries out to this Jesus for mercy. People try to silence him, but he shouts all the more loudly. Jesus calls for him and, interestingly, asks him a question: 'What do you want me to do for you?' He does not assume that he knows what the man wants, although to everybody (including us) the answer seems obvious.

For the man, the answer to this question is simple (and difficult) enough. The reason for his being pushed to the roadside of society is his blindness, so 'Lord, let me see again' is his immediate reply. Luke tells us that Jesus' response is equally immediate. The man is healed, he praises God and so does everyone who sees this amazing event.

## Reflection

*Imagine that this Jesus is asking you the same question today. 'What do you want me to do for you?' Take your time and prayerfully allow an idea to take shape in you over the day. Then make your response and let it go.*

IAN ADAMS

# Becoming present

[Jesus] entered Jericho and was passing through it. A man was there named Zacchaeus; he was a chief tax-collector and was rich. He was trying to see who Jesus was, but on account of the crowd he could not, because he was short in stature. So he ran ahead and climbed a sycamore tree to see him, because he was going to pass that way. When Jesus came to the place, he looked up and said to him, 'Zacchaeus, hurry and come down; for I must stay at your house today.' So he hurried down and was happy to welcome him.

The much-loved story of Zacchaeus only appears in Luke's Gospel and shows the skill of his storytelling. In just a few sentences, Jesus' life-changing encounter with the speculative tax-gathering Zacchaeus unfolds. It feels as if we are part of the scene and can sense both the joy and the tension that the story produces even now. We do not know all that is said or happens between them, but Jesus' presence seems to be the key factor in the change of direction that Zacchaeus decides on, rather than any words said. Jesus simply says to Zacchaeus, who has climbed a tree in his attempts to see the healer-teacher, 'Hurry and come down; for I must stay at your house today' (v. 5).

I wonder if all of our prayers are best understood as nurturing a response to the one who longs to stay with us and for us to become 'happy to welcome him' (v. 6). However we pray, whatever our preferred pattern or style, our hope is to become increasingly present to the God who is always present to us. This is liberating, but, as was the case with Zacchaeus, it may not be popular with everyone around us. Our attempts to offer and keep open house for Christ may be seen by some as presumptuous or irrelevant. Never mind: presence is what truly matters.

## Reflection

*Commit yourself today to opening up a potential encounter space with Jesus who is saying to you, 'I must stay at your house today.' Create time, and perhaps even a physical space, in which your sole intention is towards being present to him.*

IAN ADAMS

# The shouting stones

As [Jesus] was now approaching the path down from the Mount of Olives, the whole multitude of the disciples began to praise God joyfully with a loud voice for all the deeds of power that they had seen, saying, 'Blessed is the king who comes in the name of the Lord! Peace in heaven, and glory in the highest heaven!' Some of the Pharisees in the crowd said to him, 'Teacher, order your disciples to stop.' He answered, 'I tell you, if these were silent, the stones would shout out.'

Jesus is heading towards Jerusalem, famously riding on the colt of a donkey, far from royal transport (see vv. 29–35). The people, however, seem to recognise the importance of the one who is making such a humble entry into the city and shout their acclaim in words that echo the old Jewish scriptures. Some of the Pharisees present—lovers and guardians of the faith—are not impressed and tell Jesus to order the people to stop. Memorably, Jesus replies, 'I tell you, if these were silent, the stones would shout out' (v. 40). The people's praise is just the tip of something much greater.

Perhaps we can let this episode ask a question of us. What might the 'stones' be shouting out at this time? Paul talks about all creation groaning for release (Romans 8:22); the psalmists see the earth as shouting for joy (Psalm 98). Can we quieten ourselves to sense what the natural world around us is shouting, saying or singing?

This leads to a second question. What might we be shouting, saying or singing for the Christ who comes? It is helpful to see this as an open question that must begin and end in authenticity. Even if our present song is muted, if we sing it with authenticity, we may discover in time a more joyful song rising within us again that is in time and in tune with the 'shouting stones'.

### Reflection

*If you are able to do so, get out today for a walk, run, swim or cycle in the natural world. Listen out for what you sense of songs of lament and praise, and join in.*

IAN ADAMS

# Weep over it

As [Jesus] came near and saw the city, he wept over it, saying, 'If you, even you, had only recognised on this day the things that make for peace! But now they are hidden from your eyes. Indeed, the days will come upon you, when your enemies will set up ramparts around you and surround you, and hem you in on every side. They will crush you to the ground, you and your children within you, and they will not leave within you one stone upon another; because you did not recognise the time of your visitation from God.'

Jesus weeps over the city that he loves. Anticipating, perhaps, the tragedy that will unfold in AD70, when the Romans finally lay waste to Jerusalem and destroy the temple, Jesus weeps for not only the city but also its lack of understanding of what is needed to create true and lasting peace. We can imagine that he is referring to more here than the need for political nous in handling the occupying forces (although that may be important). The peaceable kingdom of God has to begin here and it has to begin with us, as individuals and as communities. On both counts, Jerusalem has, in Jesus' eyes, missed the mark.

Sometimes, inevitably, we take our own setting for granted. We can miss both its shortcomings and the many good things that happen in the locality. This episode in Luke 19 can be an encouragement to us to get out into our locality—whether it be a hamlet or a town, a village or a city—to 'come near' to it as Jesus comes near to Jerusalem, to give the place our deep attention, then let a response rise within us. We may, of course, be part of the solution to the things over which we weep, directly or indirectly.

## Reflection

*Take a leisurely walk in your setting. Pay attention to the place and its people. What calls for a joyful response? What makes you want to weep? How, if at all, do you sense that you might become part of creating God's peaceable kingdom here?*

IAN ADAMS

# An abrasive Jesus

But [Jesus] looked at [the people] and said, 'What then does this text mean: "The stone that the builders rejected has become the cornerstone"? Everyone who falls on that stone will be broken to pieces; and it will crush anyone on whom it falls.' When the scribes and chief priests realised that he had told this parable against them, they wanted to lay hands on him at that very hour, but they feared the people.

This exchange comes at the end of a longer conversation in the temple with the chief priests, the scribes and the elders. It is a public run-in with the religious authorities, which feels dangerous, but Jesus does not seem to be in the mood to calm things down. The leaders have asked Jesus to clarify by what authority he is teaching. He has outflanked this question, then told a parable about some wicked tenants cheating an absent landowner, abusing his representatives and killing his son—a parable that the leaders soon realise features them and in a very unfavourable light. Jesus then further ratchets up the atmosphere by quoting a line from the psalms, about a rejected stone becoming the cornerstone. Finally comes the punchline. Anyone who messes with the stone will themselves be crushed, broken to pieces.

What are we to make of this uncomfortable, punchy, abrasive Jesus? It is a reminder, of course, that he cannot be boxed in by any of our assumptions. He will be who he is and we must allow him to be so. It is also a reminder that there may be times when both he and we must be spirited and strong in our resistance to whatever is dehumanising and destructive. The wisdom we need is to know how and when it is necessary to do this. Spikiness in *all* things is not modelled by Jesus and is not a good strategy for a peaceable, peacemaking life. There will be moments, however, when some spikiness is called for. 'Blessed are the peacemakers' (Matthew 5:9) is always a close companion to 'Blessed are those who hunger and thirst for righteousness' (v. 6).

**Prayer**

*Jesus, compassionate and strong, help me to know how and when to resist whatever is dehumanising and destructive.*

IAN ADAMS

# To the emperor? To God?

So they asked him, 'Teacher, we know that you are right in what you say and teach, and you show deference to no one, but teach the way of God in accordance with truth. Is it lawful for us to pay taxes to the emperor, or not?' But he perceived their craftiness and said to them, 'Show me a denarius. Whose head and whose title does it bear?' They said, 'The emperor's.' He said to them, 'Then give to the emperor the things that are the emperor's, and to God the things that are God's.'

Here is another exchange featuring Jesus with the religious authorities. The temperature of the conversation seems to have dropped and there is a sense of more space around, but then comes a killer question in public from the leaders. They know that there is nowhere for Jesus to hide from this one. In the full glare of the media, as it were, he is asked whether or not it is lawful to pay taxes to the emperor. If he says yes, he will be undercutting his authority to speak as an authentic leader within the Jewish faith. If he says no, he will be risking the wrath of the Romans, who rather like taxes paid in full and on time. In a brilliant response, Jesus requests a coin, asks whose head is on the coin (the emperor's) and says, 'Then give to the emperor the things that are the emperor's, and to God the things that are God's' (v. 25).

This answer works on so many levels. It turns aside the attack on him; it sends the question back to the questioners; it gets everyone thinking about what is truly due to the emperor and what is truly due to God. The answer is actually far more radical than a simple injunction not to pay taxes to the emperor. It also raises questions about the suitability of the temple authorities to receive their own taxes. Let us drop this question into our own contexts. Today we will do all kinds of things. Who will they be for? Who is really due what?

## Reflection

*Carry a coin with you today. Every time you remember the coin, ask yourself who you are acting for in this moment.*

IAN ADAMS

# Beware of status

> In the hearing of all the people he said to the disciples, 'Beware of the scribes, who like to walk around in long robes, and love to be greeted with respect in the market-places, and to have the best seats in the synagogues and places of honour at banquets. They devour widows' houses and for the sake of appearance say long prayers. They will receive the greater condemnation.'

Chapter 20 of Luke's Gospel concludes with yet another glimpse of a Jesus who is behaving more provocatively than we might have imagined. In the hearing of everyone, says Luke, Jesus makes clear his disdain for the scribes and their love of status. We can imagine a group of scribes walking past as he says this, robes swishing as they walk, with their 'phylacteries broad and their fringes long' (Matthew 23:5). If you claim to be religious, suggests Jesus, the truthfulness of your claim is only to be found in the way that you conduct yourself. Flowing robes and obtaining the best seats may not be the problem here per se, but it is what they signify—and it is how they are obtained and used.

Going further, Jesus describes far more worrying wrongdoing, accusing the scribes of 'devouring widows' houses' (Luke 20:47). He also suggests that even the religious practice of the scribes may be bogus, with long prayers that are actually no more than deceits, designed to impress those within earshot rather than genuine attempts to engage with God.

So here is a gritty question for us as we conclude this series of readings. What is our relationship to status? To what extent are we concerned about being popular, recognised and rewarded? Is there any sign that we are people happy in companionship with the Christ, able to trust ourselves to descent and loss if that comes our way, and happy to be remembered by him alone if that is required of us? This is demanding stuff, but we are not alone. Jesus says, 'Remember, I am with you always, to the end of the age' (Matthew 28:20).

### Prayer

*Jesus—our companion, friend and Saviour—help us to walk your path of humility and love.*

IAN ADAMS

# Love and wonder: Thomas Traherne

In the winter of 1896–97, a booklover found in the bargain baskets of two separate secondhand bookshops a handful of anonymous manuscripts. They turned out to contain some poems and an unknown theological work, *Centuries of Meditation*, which were soon proved to be by the obscure 17th-century Herefordshire poet and cleric Thomas Traherne. This extraordinary work was first published in 1908, more than two centuries after Traherne's death.

*Centuries of Meditation* is an unfinished cycle of five sets of 'centuries', each (except the last) consisting of 100 short meditations. It is this masterpiece that we will be exploring. Traherne wrote it for his friend Susannah Hopton, who ran a small 'society for the study and practice of religion', and sent it to her in manuscript form. Traherne's aim was to discover the secret of what he calls 'Felicity', or happiness. He finds this in the glories of God's creation and the God who made it, rediscovering the pure vision of the beauty of the world that he had as a child. In this he is a leading light of what tradition calls the '*via positiva*'—that is, finding God in God's world and in everyday life, as opposed to the '*via negativa*', which is turning one's back on sensory experience to find God.

Both ways are needed, but the first—Traherne's way—is perhaps especially relevant for our times, when we need to learn to love God's creation so as to save it from our own destructive behaviour. It seems a miracle that his text was rediscovered in the 20th century. More extraordinary still, three more manuscripts have been found since—one, already on fire, on top of a smouldering rubbish heap in the 1960s and two hidden in libraries in the 1990s. These have since been studied and published.

To give the flavour of Traherne's thought, I have included a quotation from him each day alongside the Bible passage. This seems appropriate, as his meditations are deeply inspired by the Bible and his love for it, the God it reveals shining through every page. I have not modernised his quaint language, except in one place for comprehension.

*Veronica Zundel*

# A ready writer

Go now, write it before them on a tablet, and inscribe it in a book,
so that it may be for the time to come as a witness for ever.

*'An empty book is like an infant's soul, in which anything may be written. It
is capable of all things, but containeth nothing. I have a mind to fill this with
profitable wonders.'*

This is the opening sentence of Traherne's book. We know now what
he did not—that an 'infant's soul' is *not* a blank sheet. Babies come
with ready-made personalities and abilities, wired for language and
relationships. Nevertheless, parents will know that excited feeling of a
new, perfect person, not yet damaged by the world, and writers will
know the clean feeling of a new page ready to receive their 'pearls of
wisdom'. The artist's white canvas or the engineer's sheet of metal may
evoke similar sensations. Did God have the same feeling, looking at the
newly created world, with all its potential, not yet distorted by sin?

The Bible verse I have linked with this quote from Traherne, tells us
that what we 'write', whether that be on our children's lives, paper or a
screen or on the world, has eternal consequences. It is 'a witness forever' to the good or bad we do. In case that sounds too scary, let me
add that I believe Jesus died for our future sins as well as our past ones
and, in Christ, God's grace is always there, erasing what we have done
wrong and empowering us to do better.

'Profitable wonders': what an amazing goal to have for your writing
or other work you might do. Last night I was watching a science programme about the search for alternatives to antibiotics, now that more
and more bacteria are becoming resistant to them. The world is full of
both usefulness and glory and we have been given the ability to discover
and share both of them. We cannot all be research scientists but we can,
by our tiniest actions, show both the 'profitableness' (not necessarily
financial!) and the wonders of the world.

### Prayer

*Pray for those with children born already damaged and for those who can
find no work or no profit or wonder in the work they do.*

VERONICA ZUNDEL

GENESIS 1:29–31 (NRSV, ABRIDGED)

# Beautiful in its time

God said, 'See, I have given you every plant yielding seed that is upon the face of all the earth, and every tree with seed in its fruit; you shall have them for food'… And it was so. God saw everything that he had made, and indeed, it was very good.

*'Certainly Adam in Paradise had not more sweet and curious apprehensions of the world, than I had when I was a child… The corn was orient and immortal wheat, which never should be reaped, nor was ever sown… The green trees when I saw them first through one of the gates transported and ravished me, their sweetness and unusual beauty made my heart to leap, and almost mad with ecstasy, they were such strange and wonderful things.'*

If you have small children, have they ever ignored the expensive toy you bought them and spent hours playing in the cardboard box it came in? For a child, the smallest aspects of the world are charged with fascination. An ant on the pathway, a wooden spoon and a saucepan, all can open a whole world of imagination.

It is hard to recall the intense sensory consciousness we had as children and lost as we became toughened by the world. Artistic (and autistic) people retain it and we can all rediscover it in our spiritual experiences or by looking very carefully. Traherne had a strong memory of his childhood vision and believed that, in seeking to recover it, he was re-encountering the God who made the material world 'very good'.

God did not make us human beings as disembodied 'souls', nor will our eternal life with God be disembodied (1 Corinthians 15:42–44). Just as parents delight in seeing their children acquire physical skills, from sucking to holding to walking, so God delights in us as we use our God-given senses of sight, hearing, touch, taste and smell to explore the world.

How do you use your senses in your daily work and life? How does your church address the different senses in its worship?

## Reflection

*Choose one natural object: a tree, a flower, a shell, a piece of bread. Spend time exploring it with every sense you can. Then thank God for your senses.*

VERONICA ZUNDEL

# Precious in God's sight

When I look at your heavens, the work of your fingers, the moon and the stars that you have established; what are human beings that you are mindful of them, mortals that you care for them? Yet you have made them a little lower than God, and crowned them with glory and honour. You have given them dominion over the works of your hands; you have put all things under their feet.

*'The men! O what venerable and reverend creatures did the aged seem! Immortal cherubims! And young men glittering and sparkling angels, and maids strange seraphic pieces of life and beauty! Boys and girls tumbling in the street, and playing, were moving jewels.'*

I always feel uncomfortable when people respond to a slip-up by someone they admire, by saying, 'That's so human.' Why do we label the negative as 'human' but not the positive? Why do we not say, for instance, of the discovery of the Higgs boson, 'That's so human'? After all, it is. God has made us with an amazing capacity for learning about how God's world works and creating new things in it, such as art, poetry, music. Non-human creatures can do astounding things, but they cannot understand the world around them.

The psalmist and Traherne share a view of human beings as incredible creatures, both beautiful and intelligent, made in the image of God. That image enables us to both know and love. It is not just our 'reason' that is evidence we are made in God's image, as traditionally thought, but also our capacity for relationships and giving. Our 'dominion' over creation does not give us a right of exploitation, but a duty of care. That includes care of our fellow human beings, who are 'venerable creatures', 'strange seraphic pieces of life and beauty', 'a little lower than God'.

Whenever I see someone who has clearly been broken by life—say, a drunk on the street—I think, 'That person was once someone's infinitely precious baby.' Of course that may not always be true—the person may have been someone's unwanted and resented baby—but they were certainly God's infinitely precious and wanted baby.

### Prayer
*Pray for those whose lives have almost totally obscured the image of God.*

VERONICA ZUNDEL

# A child's-eye view

For what can be known about God is plain to them, because God has shown it to them. Ever since the creation of the world his eternal power and divine nature, invisible though they are, have been understood and seen through the things he has made. So they are without excuse; for though they knew God, they did not honour him as God or give thanks to him, but they became futile in their thinking, and their senseless minds were darkened.

*'All the world was mine, and I the only spectator and enjoyer of it. I knew no churlish properties, nor bounds, nor divisions, but all properties and divisions were mine; all treasures and the possessors of them. So that with much ado I was corrupted, and made to learn the dirty devices of this world. Which now I unlearn, and become, as it were, a little child again that I may enter into the kingdom of God.'*

The 'new atheists' argue that science's discoveries have left no room for God in the world. For myself, the more I learn (mostly from television) about new scientific discoveries, the more I think there is a God who creates and sustains this extraordinary universe, where the infinitely small mirrors the infinitely large in its complexity.

Paul echoes the Old Testament in pointing out that the physical world is an expression of the life of God, in which we can read God's goodness and power. Traherne as a child saw this clearly, for his mind had not yet grasped the idea of 'This bit of the world is mine, and not yours'. It was *all* his—and it was all God's. Humans are fallen, though, and we grow up in a society where the earth's 'treasures' are unequally divided and where we have taken God's gifts and used them in a way that harms others.

For Traherne, becoming like a child to enter the kingdom of God meant getting back to a world where God had given enough for everyone and for it to be shared with everyone. The 'dirty devices' of the world are not just sexual aberrations or crime but also greed, corruption and self-serving politics.

## Reflection

*What do you think is the number one cause of inequality in the world?*

VERONICA ZUNDEL

# The words of life

The law of the Lord is perfect, reviving the soul; the decrees of the Lord are sure, making wise the simple; the precepts of the Lord are right, rejoicing the heart... the ordinances of the Lord are true and righteous altogether. More to be desired are they than gold, even much fine gold; sweeter also than honey, and drippings of the honeycomb.

*'Among other things there befell me a most infinite desire of a book from Heaven. For observing all things to be rude and superfluous here upon earth, I thought the ways of felicity to be known only among the holy angels; and that unless I could receive information from them, I could never be happy... till at last I perceived that the God of angels had taken care of me... for he had sent the book I wanted before I was born.'*

In a celebrity-focused culture, a new book from a famous person (even if it is ghost-written) garners immediate interest from the media and the book-buying public. We think it will give us insight into the person we admire or perhaps envy.

Traherne's search was not for information but for what he called 'felicity'. It was obvious to him (though it is not always obvious to the rest of us) that study, career success or valuable possessions were not going to give him what he was looking for. Perhaps some secret revelation from angelic realms would give him the key?

It took him a while to realise that the 'secret knowledge' he sought was already in his hands, and available to everyone. In fact, the book he wanted had been written long before he came into the world and was just waiting for him to explore it.

The Bible is not our Saviour—it can and has been misused to oppress, exclude and condemn—but it is the place where we find the history of God's love affair with humankind and, above all, where we meet Jesus, the crowning gift of that love. We may need to look at it afresh to find the joy and wonder it contains.

### Prayer
*'Open my eyes, so that I may behold wondrous things out of your law'*
*(Psalm 119:18).*

VERONICA ZUNDEL

MATTHEW 6:19–21 (NRSV)

# Treasure hunt

'Do not store up for yourselves treasures on earth, where moth and rust consume and where thieves break in and steal; but store up for yourselves treasures in heaven, where neither moth nor rust consumes and where thieves do not break in and steal. For where your treasure is, there your heart will be also.'

*'I was guided by an implicit faith in God's goodness; and therefore led to the study of the most obvious and common things... For nothing is more natural to infinite goodness, than to make the best things most frequent, and only things worthless scarce. Then I began to inquire what things were most common: air, light, heaven and earth, water, the sun, trees, men and women... these I found common and obvious to all; rubies, pearl, diamonds, gold and silver; these I found scarce... and I saw clearly, that there was a real valuableness in the common things; in the scarce, a feigned.'*

Yesterday on the radio I heard that the so-called 'rare' earth elements vital for modern technology are not rare at all. Why do we value something so much more if it is hard to come by? In Sir Thomas More's imaginary world 'Utopia', children laugh at the mayor wearing a big gold chain round his neck as, in their culture, gold is a worthless plaything and only fools wear it.

Traherne had much the same idea. What we should value most are the essentials of our lives: water, air, plants. As God has given us so many of them, they must be the most important things. If Traherne had lived today, he would certainly be campaigning to save the rainforests. He includes people in his list: God must really like people, he made so many!

Accumulating 'treasures in heaven' does not necessarily mean turning our backs on the physical world as it is impossible to do completely without dying. It may mean valuing what God values, working to make sure everyone has enough to eat, for example.

### Reflection

*One way to store heavenly treasure is to do the best we can with what we have been given to share on earth.*

VERONICA ZUNDEL

# Two worlds

For God so loved the world that he gave his only Son, so that everyone who believes in him may not perish but may have eternal life. Indeed, God did not send the Son into the world to condemn the world, but in order that the world might be saved through him... Do not love the world or the things in the world. The love of the Father is not in those who love the world; for all that is in the world—the desire of the flesh, the desire of the eyes, the pride in riches—comes not from the Father but from the world.

*'To contemn the world and to enjoy the world are things contrary to each other. How then can we contemn the world, which we are born to enjoy? Truly there are two worlds. One was made by God, the other by men. That made by God was great and beautiful... That made by men is a Babel of confusions.'*

So, God loves the world, but we are not to do likewise? I am confused. Looking at the Greek does not help me either: the same word, *kosmos*, is used for 'world' in both passages. I think Traherne solves the puzzle for us here.

'The world' can mean the physical creation, the universe God made for his own pleasure and ours, but it can also mean what old hippies call 'the man', what today we would call 'the system'. This is the social and political order we have created—an order full of greed, oppression, exclusion and hatred. This (and its products of wealth for some and poverty for others) we are not to love.

All the good gifts of creation come from 'the Father' (James 1:17), but our overconsumption in the developed world is based on the deprivation of others. Aiming to be 'the most competitive nation' means some other nations are going to lose out in this human-made race.

Nevertheless, we are not called to 'contemn', to use Traherne's word, any part of the world, rich or poor. Our task is not to judge (Matthew 7:1), but to perform 'the ministry of reconciliation' (2 Corinthians 5:18–19).

## Prayer

*Pray for a more just world.*

VERONICA ZUNDEL

2 CORINTHIANS 5:19–21 (NRSV, ABRIDGED)

# Crux of the matter

In Christ God was reconciling the world to himself, not counting their trespasses against them, and entrusting the message of reconciliation to us... For our sake he made him to be sin who knew no sin, so that in him we might become the righteousness of God.

*'The Cross of Christ is the Jacob's ladder by which we ascend into the highest heavens... That Cross is a tree set on fire with invisible flame, that illumina-teth all the world. The flame is love: the love in his bosom who died on it... Why Lord Jesus, does thou love men: why are they all thy treasures? What wonder is this, that thou shouldest so esteem them as to die for them? Show me the treasures of thy love, that I may love them too.'*

Some years ago, I wrote a Bible reading note in which I said, 'I do not know how the cross "works".' In response, I got a letter from a fellow writer who said my comment had liberated her from years of trying to understand the cross a certain way, which had never made sense for her.

The Bible uses many different images to 'explain' how the cross affects us—the law court, marriage, religious sacrifice and, here, a kind of 'exchange mechanism'. All of these images must have made sense for the first hearers of the New Testament letters. Some still resonate with us, but others are harder to grasp: after all, animal sacrifice is no longer a part of our daily lives. Thank God we are not saved by understanding the cross a particular way. What we do know is that Jesus' life and death have freed us from 'the system' that we looked at yesterday and called and enabled us to live new lives.

Traherne did not put forward a new understanding of the cross. He just sees it as a ladder between earth and heaven, flaming with the passionate love of God for humanity. His response is the desire to love his fellow humans as God loves them. If this is not our response, too, then maybe we do not understand the cross at all.

### Reflection

*What does it mean to you to 'become the righteousness of God'?*

VERONICA ZUNDEL

# The centre of the world

He is the image of the invisible God, the firstborn of all creation; for in him all things in heaven and on earth were created, things visible and invisible... all things have been created through him and for him. He himself is before all things, and in him all things hold together.

*'The world serves you, as it teaches you more abundantly to prize the love of Jesus Christ. For since the inheritance is so great to which you are restored, and no less than the whole world is the benefit of your Saviour's love, how much are you to admire that person that redeemed you from the lowest Hell to the fruition of it?'*

Recently I had a debate with a fellow Christian on Facebook. The topic was my assertion that under the surface of much Christian thinking today lurks the heresy of Manichaeanism. Manichaeans believed there were two equal Gods, one good and one evil, and that it was the evil one who had created matter. Salvation meant escaping from matter into pure spirit.

Now, of course, modern Christians do not believe God has an evil twin, but many seem to believe (contrary to what the Bible actually teaches) that God is planning to scrap this physical world and whisk us off to an ethereal realm called heaven. Such beliefs have consequences. If you think God is finished with the material world, you certainly will not bother to take the measures we need to save it.

For Jesus himself, however, knowing God did not turn him away from the material world. On the contrary, he looked closely at it—wild flowers growing, birds hopping on and off branches, women baking bread, shepherds rescuing sheep—and out of these everyday events he made his stories of challenge, forgiveness and grace. You could say, as Thomas Hardy said of himself, 'he was a man who used to notice such things'.

Then, why would he not, as he was the creator of them? Traherne reminds us that the material world is not a distraction from Jesus. It is what reveals Jesus to us.

### Prayer

*Pray that governments and individuals will act to save the beautiful earth God made.*

VERONICA ZUNDEL

COLOSSIANS 1:19–20 (NRSV)

# Bring 'em all in

For in him all the fullness of God was pleased to dwell, and through him God was pleased to reconcile to himself all things, whether on earth or in heaven, by making peace through the blood of his cross.

*'And now, O Lord, Heaven and Earth are infinitely more valuable than they were before, being all bought with Thy precious blood. And thou, O Jesus, art a treasure unto me far greater than all those… Lord, I lament and abhor myself that I have been the occasion of these thy sufferings. I had never known the dignity of my nature, hadst not thou esteemed it; I had never seen or understood its glory, hadst thou not assumed it.'*

The now defunct US Christian magazine *The Other Side* had a feature called 'The Reversed Standard Version'. They took a well-known Bible passage and subtly altered it so that it said what the world, or sometimes some Christians, appeared to believe. It was a punchy way of focusing on what it really says.

Were I to do a 'reversed standard version' on this passage from Colossians, it might read like this: 'Through him God was pleased to reconcile to himself some people, and take them from earth to heaven.' In fact, the writer of Colossians tells us God's plan is to reconcile 'all things', a phrase he repeatedly uses and one that also pops up in several other places in the New Testament.

If this is so, then why do we speak and act as if God is only interested in saving people? Have we not noticed that in our favourite evangelistic verse, John 3:16, we are told Jesus came 'in order that the world might be saved through him' (v. 17)? There is no doubt in the New Testament that God's innermost desire is to transform not only all people but also the damaged, yet incredible, world they live in. At a recent festival worship service, I sang a moving song with the repeated chorus 'Bring 'em all in'. Actually, though, our mission is to reconcile people not only to God but also the world.

## Reflection

*'In Christ God was reconciling the world to himself… and entrusting the message of reconciliation to us' (2 Corinthians 5:19).*

VERONICA ZUNDEL

# The way we were

God blessed them, and God said to them, 'Be fruitful and multiply, and fill the earth and subdue it; and have dominion over the fish of the sea and over the birds of the air and over every living thing that moves upon the earth.'

*'Till you see that the world is yours, you cannot weigh the greatness of sin, nor the misery of your fall, nor prize your redeemer's love… For the greatness of sin proceedeth from the greatness of his love whom we have offended, from the greatness of those obligations which were laid upon us, from the great blessedness and glory of the estate wherein we were placed.'*

'Human nature'. What does that phrase mean to you? Probably something to do with our weakness, our tendency to mess up our or other people's best efforts, our propensity to be self-centred, greedy, bullying. Human nature is also glorious, though, as it is made in the image of God (Genesis 1:26) and it is the nature Jesus that took upon himself to redeem. In yesterday's quote from Traherne we read, 'I had never known the dignity of my nature, hadst not Thou esteemed it.' Humanity is both hallowed by its Creator and honoured by its Redeemer.

In the light of 'the great blessedness and glory of the estate wherein we were placed'—our status and calling in creation—our sin does indeed look greater. Instead of caring for the earth, we have exploited and dominated it; instead of loving and respecting our fellow human beings, we have oppressed them or turned our backs on their need.

What does Traherne mean by 'the world is yours'? I do not think it means quite the same as the phrase 'the world's your oyster'. The world is not ours to do with as we please, but it is ours to enjoy and develop—under God's direction. The love with which God gave us the creation is the same love with which Jesus died, love that sets us free to do right.

### Reflection

*Is God delighted every time humanity discovers something new about God's world?*

VERONICA ZUNDEL

# Where God lives

Jacob... came to a certain place and stayed there for the night... And he dreamed that there was a ladder set up on the earth, the top of it reaching to heaven; and the angels of God were ascending and descending on it... Then Jacob woke from his sleep and said, 'Surely the Lord is in this place—and I did not know it!... How awesome is this place! This is none other than the house of God, and this is the gate of heaven.'

*'You never enjoy the world aright, till the sea itself floweth in your veins, till you are clothed with the heavens, and crowned with the stars; and perceive yourself to be the sole heir of the whole world, and more than so, because men are in it who are every one sole heirs as well as you. Till you can sing and rejoice and delight in God, as misers do in gold, and kings in sceptres, you never enjoy the world.'*

People used to refer to church buildings as 'the house of God' and, consequently, many are lavish and beautifully decorated. Solomon's temple, decked with precious metals, furnished with rare woods and luxurious fabrics, must have been mind-blowing. It is not in our physical buildings that God lives, however, and Solomon himself acknowledged this: 'Even heaven and the highest heaven cannot contain you, much less this house that I have built!' (1 Kings 8:27). The temple and our church buildings are just symbols for the reality that God is with us everywhere, from supernovas to the smallest atom. The answer to Solomon's question is 'Yes, God will dwell on earth', not only in Jesus, who acts as a lens focusing God's presence, but in everything that exists and lives.

Traherne's vision of oneness with creation is also a vision of oneness in God: as we delight in the sea, the stars, the whole earth, we are also delighting in their Creator. 'Enjoying the world' in this sense is not a sin, it is a way of praying.

**Prayer**

*Teach me to love your creation not only because it is wonderful
but also because it is yours.*

Veronica Zundel

# Woman alive

A capable wife who can find? She is far more precious than jewels... Her children rise up and call her happy; her husband too, and he praises her: 'Many women have done excellently, but you surpass them all.' Charm is deceitful, and beauty is vain, but a woman who fears the Lord is to be praised. Give her a share in the fruit of her hands, and let her works praise her in the city gates.

*'Suppose a curious and fair woman. Some have seen the beauties of Heaven in such a person. It is a vain thing to say they loved too much… They loved it not too much, but upon false causes… They love a creature for sparkling eyes and curled hair, lily breasts and ruddy cheeks; which they should love moreover for being God's Image, Queen of the Universe, beloved by Angels, redeemed by Jesus Christ, an heiress of Heaven, and temple of the Holy Ghost.'*

We have a new Avon lady in our area and I have been succumbing to face creams, scented shower gels and new lipsticks! When I look in the mirror, though, I know none of these things will reverse the march of time across my face, leaving its marks.

There is nothing wrong with looking good, but thank God that women are not (or should not be) valued for their looks in God's kingdom. Proverbs 31 is a passage that some women love to hate, with its impossible standard of running a home and a business, doing charitable work, rising early and staying up late making crafts. Its redeeming feature, however, is that it values this imaginary wife (and she is imaginary) not for her pretty face but for her achievements in serving God. That is a relief for those of us who are never going to be a perfect 10!

Traherne's attitude to the equality of women is not only biblical but also very radical for his time. I think today he would be in the forefront of Christian feminism!

## Reflection

*'Give her a share in the fruit of her hands, and let her works praise her in the city gates' (v. 31). What does this say about women's pay and prospects in the workplace?*

VERONICA ZUNDEL

# Love unlimited

Then the king will say to those at his right hand, 'Come, you that are blessed by my Father, inherit the kingdom prepared for you from the foundation of the world; for I was hungry and you gave me food, I was thirsty and you gave me something to drink, I was a stranger and you welcomed me, I was naked and you gave me clothing, I was sick and you took care of me, I was in prison and you visited me.

*'Shall I not love him infinitely for whom God made the world and gave his Son?… Examine yourself well, and you will find it a difficult matter to love God so as to die for him, and not to love your brother so as to die for him in like manner. Shall I not love him infinitely whom God loveth infinitely, and commendeth to my love, as the representative of himself, with such a saying, "What ye do to him is done unto Me"?'*

Sometimes I think I am not a proper Christian. If you read biographies of Christians in some heroic or dangerous ministry, you can wonder whether you, in your small corner, are doing anything for God. After all, Jesus does not say, 'I needed a book and you wrote it' or even 'My bed needed changing and you changed it.' What real use am I?

Neither does he say, though, 'You solved world hunger' or 'You eradicated malaria.' If we help just one person in need, we are doing what Jesus has called us to. 'To love your brother so as to die for him', as Traherne puts it, may not mean literally dying, but a daily 'dying to self' for the sake of whatever others God has placed around us.

'Those who do not love a brother or sister whom they have seen, cannot love God whom they have not seen,' says 1 John 4:20. Sometimes I find it harder to love some of my sisters and brothers in God than to love a complete stranger. It is always hardest to get on with the members of your own family, but it is the only way to love God.

### Prayer
*Lord, teach us to love as you love us.*

VERONICA ZUNDEL

# Harvest

When I was asked to write on a harvest theme, I immediately thought of all the things that go with a traditional harvest festival—readings about baskets of good things, songs about golden fields and church windowsills covered with apples. This may well be your response, too!

Then, as I am someone who always takes an interest in history and in how the customs of a culture grow and develop, I thought I would take a look way back in the past, to the beginnings of the Old Testament and see what lessons we could learn from it to help our thinking about harvest.

First, we find warnings about getting too comfortable in times of prosperity, a message to which we should have been paying a lot more attention today. Then, as now, however, whether times are good or bad, it is always the right time to learn to trust God rather than worry about our own needs. God, who made the beautiful flowers that Jesus must have been looking at during the Sermon on the Mount, cares about us.

When we turn to some of the parables Jesus told, we should remember that his world was very different from ours, although we recognise some of the everyday things he talked about, such as seeds being sown. Bread, as now, was a staple in the diet of the people then and Jesus called himself 'living bread', a new idea that the people found very hard to even begin to understand. Jesus also asked his disciples to live out the gospel message as they spent time among the people and, when he sent them out to share the news of the kingdom of God, he told them that this would be a kind of harvest of humanity.

Jesus also talked to his followers about the future, the world to come—the promise that one day everything will be made new, when the final harvest of the world takes place at the end of the age.

Individually, we are part of the big picture, but we also bear responsibility for the harvest of our own hearts. So we pray: 'Lord of the Harvest, grant that, at the end, the store house of our lives may be found to be full of good things.'

*Heather Fenton*

# When you have settled in...

When you have entered the land the Lord your God is giving you
as an inheritance and have taken possession of it and settled in
it, take some of the firstfruits of all that you produce from the soil
of the land the Lord your God is giving you and put them in a
basket. Then go to the place that the Lord your God will choose
as a dwelling for his Name and say to the priest in office at the
time, 'I declare today to the Lord your God that I have come to the
land the Lord swore to our ancestors to give us.' The priest shall
take the basket from your hands and set it down in front of the
altar of the Lord your God.

We begin our thinking about harvest by taking a traditional harvest-
themed reading that you may well hear at a church service. If it is very
familiar to you, it may even feel rather old-fashioned, possibly reminding you of being a child and carefully carrying a box or bag of fruit and
vegetables up to the front of the church or classroom to give to your
vicar or teacher.

What may be in the past for you was, of course, in the future for the
people who first heard these words. They had yet to enter the land that
God had promised them, let alone learn how to live there. It was going
to be exciting growing crops in their new homeland for the first time,
but the thrill of that was not to distract them from the need to give
thanks to God. First and foremost, they were to offer thanksgiving for
what the land would produce, but implicit in that was the thanksgiving
due for having the land itself. So here God gives his people practical
guidance in how to express their gratitude.

### Reflection

*What do we offer to God and what does it mean to us? If you are a
gardener, would you offer your prize vegetables as thanksgiving to God at
the harvest celebrations—or would you be inclined to take the ones that
would probably not win anything at the local show?*

HEATHER FENTON

# Beware of prosperity

When you have eaten and are satisfied, praise the Lord your God for the good land he has given you. Be careful that you do not forget the Lord your God, failing to observe his commands, his laws and his decrees that I am giving you this day. Otherwise, when you eat and are satisfied, when you build fine houses and settle down, and when your herds and flocks grow large and your silver and gold increase and all you have is multiplied, then your heart will become proud and you will forget the Lord your God.

'Money! Money! All will be well if we just have more money!' is the cry of our age. Wait a minute, though: money so often seems to go hand in hand with short memories and tight-fisted behaviour. In our passage today we can see that God anticipates such reactions. He warns the people that they will be in danger of forgetting that it was he who gave them all the good things they have and may start to think they achieved everything themselves. To make matters worse, they may even start worshipping other gods, which, God goes on to warn, will result in their destruction (Deuteronomy 8:20).

All this may well sound horribly familiar. As a society, we have almost completely forgotten God. We do not acknowledge the Lord, who put us in a lovely world with many resources; instead, we attribute our success to ourselves. God warned his people long ago and now, in our slick modern world, that the ability to achieve continuous growth and ongoing prosperity would be called into question. Indeed, the global economy has more questions than answers to give, but still people do not seek the living God.

We need to learn to live as Christians. We can consider what our own attitude is—how should we behave towards individuals and those whose standard of living is nothing like as good as ours, even if we feel we are in a tight corner ourselves.

**Prayer**

*Lord, keep my heart from growing proud and do not let me forget you.*

HEATHER FENTON

LUKE 12:27–32 (NIV)

# But do not worry

[Jesus said] 'Consider how the wild flowers grow. They do not labour or spin. Yet I tell you, not even Solomon in all his splendour was dressed like one of these. If that is how God clothes the grass of the field, which is here today, and tomorrow is thrown into the fire, how much more will he clothe you—you of little faith! And do not set your heart on what you will eat or drink; do not worry about it. For the pagan world runs after all such things, and your Father knows that you need them. But seek his kingdom, and these things will be given to you as well. Do not be afraid, little flock, for your Father has been pleased to give you the kingdom.'

Jesus is talking here about small but wonderful and fragile flowers that have a short life growing in the wild. He says that they look even more splendid than the famous King Solomon, who would have worn purple or possibly even white clothes, which were even more expensive!

Jesus then goes on to tell his listeners not to be afraid about the future, but to trust God the Father, who knows that they need clothes as well as food and drink. He exhorts them, instead of worrying about these things, to seek the kingdom of God first and foremost. In doing this, he says, although they are in some ways small and fearful, God will give them his very kingdom. In the same way, if the harvest of our lives is formed by seeking the kingdom of God as our priority, it will be much more wonderful than splendid clothes or even beautiful flowers.

## Reflection

*For us the idea of the kingdom of God may seem large and difficult to understand, but we need to remember that Jesus ends this section of teaching by telling us that we are not to give in to fear, because the Father is actually pleased to give us his kingdom.*

HEATHER FENTON

# Everything comes from God

[David prayed] 'But who am I, and who are my people, that we should be able to give as generously as this? Everything comes from you, and we have given you only what comes from your hand.'

David spoke these words at the end of his long life. By and large he had been faithful to God, even if he had some distinctly shaky moments! On Sunday, we looked at the people of God anticipating entering the promised land. Now they are well settled there and they have had David's excellent leadership, but they still do not have a temple as a focal point for worship. David's deepest desire is 'to build a house as a place of rest for the ark of the covenant of the Lord' (28:2), but his son is to have this privilege.

The temple was to be the permanent place where rituals essential to their worship would take place and become the focus for worship over many future generations. David was not allowed to see it, but he did see the money, precious metals and jewels, and he knew that 'the people rejoiced at the willing response of their leaders, for they had given freely and wholeheartedly to the Lord' (29:9). This meant that he was able to die contented at a 'good old age' (v. 28).

Sometimes we may not be able to see something we greatly long for. It may be, for example, that God is calling us to move on from where we are when we have waited for years for change. Then, just when it is all about to happen, we can only hear about it from others.

This story focuses on different types of harvest. As well as the harvest of David's life, we see the 'harvest' of possessions, collected over many years, being used willingly for the glory of God, creating something new and of great importance as the answer to many prayers in God's good time.

### Prayer

*Thank you, Lord, that everything comes from you—not just the fruits of the land and sea but also my own life and possessions, all given by your generous hand. Give me the grace to share these things as and when you ask me.*

HEATHER FENTON

# Jesus, the living bread

Then Jesus declared, 'I am the bread of life. Whoever comes to me will never go hungry, and whoever believes in me will never be thirsty. But as I told you, you have seen me and still you do not believe. All those the Father gives me will come to me, and whoever comes to me I will never drive away. For I have come down from heaven not to do my will but to do the will of him who sent me. And this is the will of him who sent me, that I shall lose none of all those he has given me, but raise them up at the last day.'

As we focus on food for harvest, it is worth remembering that of all the possible food we have these days, bread is still one of the basics. Today, as we live in a 'global village', it may also be quite easy to obtain and enjoy many different and exotic types of bread. In this passage, though, Jesus is not talking about even the most exotic bread; he is talking about himself as the 'living bread'. In verse 51 he goes so far as to say that 'whoever eats this bread will live for ever', adding that if they do not, they will have no life within them (v. 53)! Some of his disciples are very startled by these words and 'many' (v. 66) stopped following him after this.

You are probably used to hearing phrases like 'you are what you eat' as part of campaigns to get people to eat more healthily. It is of course true that whatever we eat actually becomes part of us and what becomes part of us forms what we are in many ways. Similarly, by receiving the 'living bread' that is Jesus, we make Jesus himself part of us and ourselves part of him. Feeding on Jesus via his word and the sacraments is a lifelong commitment that is even more important than our instinct to feed ourselves.

### Prayer

*Lord, help us to receive your life into ours, that we may be raised up on the last day and live for ever.*

HEATHER FENTON

# Sowing comes before reaping

Sow righteousness for yourselves, reap the fruit of unfailing love, and break up your unploughed ground; for it is time to seek the Lord, until he comes and showers his righteousness on you.

Living in the countryside as I do means that it is easy to notice how the agricultural seasons progress. Living in a more urban setting, it can be harder to have much sense at all of when the different types of work are happening out in the fields, apart from what we may see on the television or internet.

It is a cycle, one that always begins with the ground being broken up before sowing can happen. Modern machinery means that it will take one worker a day to do what would have taken a number of people quite a few days to achieve in Hosea's time. Then as now, however, farming is a real work of commitment requiring lots of time and energy.

Ploughing involves opening up the earth, getting rid of the old and exposing to the wind, rain and sun what has been brought up to the surface. Only then can the seed be sown. After that comes a long period of waiting and watching, hoping that the crop will grow and there will be a good harvest. Nothing in this process can be taken for granted and even one spell of extreme weather may make all the difference. Also, it is only at the end of the whole cycle that the harvest can happen, but, if the farmer has been stingy with his seed, sowing it too thinly or buying poor-quality seeds in order to save money, the outcome will be noticeable to even the casual passer-by.

Hosea sees ploughing as 'a time to seek the Lord', to work the barren places in our lives. An uncomfortable time of change or challenge could be seen as ploughing time, as an opportunity for God to plant new ideas and possibilities for growth in our lives. So, sow plenty of good seed into ground that has been ploughed well!

## Reflection

*'Remember this: whoever sows sparingly will also reap sparingly, and whoever sows generously will also reap generously'* (2 Corinthians 9:6).

HEATHER FENTON

MARK 4:3–8 (NIV)

# The parable of the sower

[Jesus said] 'Listen! A farmer went out to sow his seed. As he was scattering the seed, some fell along the path, and the birds came and ate it up. Some fell on rocky places, where it did not have much soil. It sprang up quickly, because the soil was shallow. But when the sun came up, the plants were scorched, and they withered because they had no root. Other seed fell among thorns, which grew up and choked the plants, so that they did not bear grain. Still other seed fell on good soil. It came up, grew and produced a crop, some multiplying thirty, some sixty, some a hundred times.'

If you have any interest in gardening, you will know that soil is not all the same. Once I lived in a place where roses grew very well. Now the soil in my garden is very stony and only a few plants seem at home there. Jesus clearly knows this as he talks of a farmer who has land with both good and poor soil. He paints a picture of the seed being scattered on all the land rather than only the more promising parts. As a result, the seed falls on the path, among the thorn bushes and even among the big stones beside the path as well as in the good soil. Thus, the harvest is patchy. As might be expected, the seed that falls on good soil does best, but even there the quality of the harvest varies from reasonable to excellent.

Later, Jesus' disciples want an explanation of the parable and he tells them that the seed is the word of God (vv. 15–20). He shows them that what happens to the seed can help them understand the different responses people make when they hear the word. God scatters his seeds everywhere, but they do not always take root. Experience tells us that what Jesus says is true. Even when the seed of the word falls on hearts that are 'good soil', there is no guarantee of a bountiful harvest.

### Prayer

*Lord, you said that people could hear but not understand what you were saying. Give us grace to understand and respond that we may be like the good soil, bearing fruit for you.*

HEATHER FENTON

# 'An enemy did this'

Jesus told them another parable: 'The kingdom of heaven is like a man who sowed good seed in his field. But while everyone was sleeping, his enemy came and sowed weeds among the wheat, and went away. When the wheat sprouted and formed heads, then the weeds also appeared. The owner's servants came to him and said, "Sir, didn't you sow good seed in your field? Where then did the weeds come from?" "An enemy did this," he replied. The servants asked him, "Do you want us to go and pull them up?" "No," he answered, "because while you are pulling the weeds, you may uproot the wheat with them. Let both grow together until the harvest. At that time I will tell the harvesters: First collect the weeds and tie them in bundles to be burned; then gather the wheat and bring it into my barn."'

Here is another picture of farming in Jesus' time. This time the field has good soil and is planted with good seed. The owner is obviously well off, with men working for him. When they discover that there are weeds growing among the good plants, they are horrified and go and tell their boss. The owner does not sound surprised. Maybe he knows he has an enemy. Anyway, he remains cool and collected and decides to leave everything as it is until harvest comes, because pulling up the weeds might end up destroying some of the crop. This means that he and his employees now have to wait until harvest to sort things out. Then, the work will be done in an orderly manner and the plants produced by the work of the enemy will be burnt on a bonfire while the good crop will be put into the barn as originally intended.

This is a picture of the harvest of the world that will happen at the end of time. Those who oppose God until that time will be allowed to continue. Then, that which is good, from God and fruitful and true will be kept and the rest rejected.

### Prayer

*Lord, let us trust your timing for the harvest.*

HEATHER FENTON

# Expect an early harvest

'My food,' said Jesus, 'is to do the will of him who sent me and to finish his work. Don't you have a saying, "It's still four months until harvest"? I tell you, open your eyes and look at the fields! They are ripe for harvest. Even now the one who reaps draws a wage and harvests a crop for eternal life, so that the sower and the reaper may be glad together. Thus the saying "One sows and another reaps" is true. I sent you to reap what you have not worked for. Others have done the hard work, and you have reaped the benefits of their labour.'

Jesus' disciples have just been shopping, leaving him to rest by a well. When they return, they find him talking to a woman. Nothing startling there for us, but, to his disciples, it was very shocking as Jewish men did not talk to Samaritan women. Jesus, however, is more interested in doing God's will than being the equivalent of what in his world would and would not have been 'politically correct'.

The conversation he had with the woman turns out to have been very significant for her and a large number of Samaritan people come to believe in Jesus as a result of what he said to her. They end up inviting Jesus to spend two days with them and then come to believe because they had heard him for themselves (vv. 39–42). These people are ready to listen, or 'ripe for harvest', as Jesus puts it (v. 35). Their coming to faith is not something that will come to fruition in the future: it is happening right there and then.

Jesus uses this opportunity to expand his disciples' thinking—and not just about who is ready to hear the good news of the kingdom of God. He points out to them that the person who initially sows the word of God into the heart and mind of another may not be the same person who is there when that word develops into a mature understanding of faith.

## Reflection

*Some are called to sow and others to reap, but both are essential and neither is better than the other. Doing the will of God is what is important.*

HEATHER FENTON

# The workers are few

Jesus went through all the towns and villages, teaching in their synagogues, proclaiming the good news of the kingdom and healing every disease and sickness. When he saw the crowds, he had compassion on them, because they were harassed and helpless, like sheep without a shepherd. Then he said to his disciples, 'The harvest is plentiful but the workers are few. Ask the Lord of the harvest, therefore, to send out workers into his harvest field.'

Today Jesus is with a whole crowd of people who are feeling 'harassed and helpless' (v. 36), lacking any sense of direction. They come from all sorts of circumstances and with many different needs, asking for help. He knows that the resources he has are a handful of followers who have not even been learning from him for very long. Jesus has two complementary ways of tackling the problem: prayer for more workers and, in the meanwhile, making good use of those he already has. His next move will be to send out the newly formed discipleship group with some basic instructions on how to do the job.

These days we may not use the image of 'sheep without a shepherd' (v. 36) ourselves, but the idea behind the image is all too familiar. We see people walking along the street, in our neighbourhood, our shops, our factories and offices, in the park, out and about, who lack any sense of direction. What is the solution? Well, in many ways it is the same as it was in Jesus' day, with us as the disciples, working in a team, going out with minimal resources and on a steep learning curve. Yes, there is still a harvest and it has now become our responsibility. We do not have to try tackling everyone at once, however. As we learned yesterday, in the story of Jesus meeting the woman at the well, one at a time will do!

## Prayer

*Lord, your disciples had not been with you very long when you put this big challenge in front of them. We ask you, Lord of the harvest, to continue to send out workers and, yes, if you will show us how, we are willing to be among them.*

HEATHER FENTON

# Creation looks to God

He makes grass grow for the cattle, and plants for people to culti-vate—bringing forth food from the earth: wine that gladdens human hearts, oil to make their faces shine, and bread that sus-tains their hearts... How many are your works, Lord! In wisdom you made them all; the earth is full of your creatures. There is the sea, vast and spacious, teeming with creatures beyond number—living things both large and small. There the ships go to and fro, and Leviathan, which you formed to frolic there. All creatures look to you to give them their food at the proper time. When you give it to them, they gather it up; when you open your hand, they are satisfied with good things.

Last year I had the holiday of a lifetime, visiting Magdalena Fjord on Svalbard in the High Arctic. It was cold but very beautiful. To get there, we crossed vast tracts of very solid-looking sea that was only just above freezing. The second part of today's Bible passage reminded me of that holiday because, despite not seeing much evidence of it 'teeming with sea creatures' (v. 25), I found this apparently pristine part of creation wonderful. We were sad to learn, however, that pollution travelling up to the region from the rest of the world is a serious issue and problems are caused by the loss of summer ice due to global warming.

Our harvest thinking ought to include reflection on what we are doing to our planet, partly because we are too greedy about what we take and unconcerned about what we leave. Not everyone can see the wilder parts of creation, but, like the psalmist, we can rejoice in what is around us. Indeed, our lack of awe may contribute to the casual way we treat our planet. We must cultivate a sense of wonder at the world as well as think about what we are doing to it. What could happen if greed and neglect were replaced with awe and wonder?

## Prayer

*Lord, your many works and the wisdom that called them into being are indeed wonderful. May our wonder transform how we see what we harvest from the earth and how we share your creation with other creatures.*

HEATHER FENTON

# Creation celebrates

The whole earth is filled with awe at your wonders; where morning dawns, where evening fades, you call forth songs of joy. You care for the land and water it; you enrich it abundantly. The streams of God are filled with water to provide the people with grain, for so you have ordained it. You drench its furrows and level its ridges; you soften it with showers and bless its crops. You crown the year with your bounty, and your carts overflow with abundance. The grasslands of the wilderness overflow; the hills are clothed with gladness. The meadows are covered with flocks and the valleys are mantled with grain; they shout for joy and sing.

Just as there is great beauty in creation, so there is great diversity. On my trip north, we visited an island in southern Norway with some sub-tropical vegetation, which contrasted with Svalbard where there were just small low-growing plants and no trees. In the passage, as the psalmist looks around where he is, he sees the diversity in his own area and thinks of it as giving glory to God.

The place where we see biodiversity most frequently may actually be the supermarket. All kinds of products from very different parts of the world clamour for our attention. We may start to feel flustered about what to choose, but, instead, we could thank God for such diversity, which offers us such choice, and remember that this is only a small portion of the huge number of varieties of even basic foods in the world.

We can also honour him by using well what we buy—for example, keeping an eye on 'use by' dates so that we do not let food go to waste. 'Sustainable' local products are good, too; indeed, we need to support agriculture in our own country, especially as producers struggle with issues of climate change. It is also important to consider buying Fair-trade products from parts of the world that grow foodstuff we cannot produce at home, to help those people who depend on exports to earn their living rather than being exploited.

## Reflection

*On your next trip to the supermarket, take a look at what our wonderfully diverse world gives us. Whether fresh, tinned, frozen or preserved, remember that it all reflects God's wonderfully diverse creation.*

HEATHER FENTON

# God cares for us in the bad times

Some time later the brook dried up because there had been no rain in the land. Then the word of the Lord came to him: 'Go at once to Zarephath in the region of Sidon and stay there. I have directed a widow there to supply you with food.' So he went to Zarephath. When he came to the town gate, a widow was there gathering sticks. He called to her and asked, 'Would you bring me a little water in a jar so I may have a drink?' As she was going to get it, he called, 'And bring me, please, a piece of bread.'

The woman whom Elijah the prophet meets is in great difficulty. The famine means that all she has left is a handful of flour and a little oil. Elijah asks for food, but reassures her that if she gives him it, God will not let her starve. Going against common sense, she makes a tiny loaf and discovers that trusting in God is more effective than waiting for rain (vv. 15–16)! Elijah stays with her and her young son and there is enough food every day for all of them; the supplies do not run out. Interestingly, however, the woman needs a second miracle, in which Elijah rescues her son from death, to convince her that he is really a man of God and that 'the word of the Lord from your mouth is the truth' (v. 24).

Through this story we learn that trusting in God is more important than using common sense. This is a hard but important lesson in a time of economic difficulties, even if we do not quite reach the level of desperation that this woman experienced. She does not get more, but what she has is not reduced. Somehow, in a way that goes entirely against common sense, her circumstances prove to be different. She never reaches the end of God's provision.

### Reflection

*God is faithful to his promise and provides the essentials, but it seems that he needs the obedience of both Elijah and the woman before his provision can take effect. What may God be asking us to do that does not make sense?*

HEATHER FENTON

# Harvesting the earth

I looked, and there before me was a white cloud, and seated on the cloud was one like a son of man with a crown of gold on his head and a sharp sickle in his hand. Then another angel came out of the temple and called in a loud voice to him who was sitting on the cloud, 'Take your sickle and reap, because the time to reap has come, for the harvest of the earth is ripe.' So he who was seated on the cloud swung his sickle over the earth, and the earth was harvested.

Revelation is full of strange pictures that people have always struggled to understand. We are back to the reaping images we looked at a few days ago about seed coming to fruition in different circumstances, with very different results, but here we are looking at the harvest of all harvests at the end of time itself. Then the reapers sent to harvest the earth will be angels who have been in the presence of God and under his control. At that time, a time still to come, everything will be sorted out and good and evil seen to be clearly separated. In the midst of all this we see that the one described as 'a son of man', seated on the cloud with a gold crown and a sharp sickle, is, in fact, Jesus. In the Gospels he often referred to himself as 'the Son of Man', but now everyone will know that he is both king and judge.

Living in the light of this is hard. Through Christ, who is both saviour from sin and judge of the world, we will receive forgiveness from, and reconciliation with, God the Father. This does not mean that we can live now just as we wish, however. Furthermore, we need to pray and work against the evils that surround us and everything which seeks to deny the lordship of Christ.

### Prayer

*Father, may I appreciate this world and everything that I have now. May I learn to listen and understand your truth so that, through Christ, I too may see the coming of the kingdom of heaven in all its fullness.*

HEATHER FENTON

# Remembering for the future:
# Deuteronomy

This book is both complicated and simple. How it came to be in its present form is complicated and there is no agreed answer, but its themes are simple and often repeated. Reading it can be a bit like listening to an elderly relative reminiscing: the same stories and themes keep coming up and, after a while, you can probably repeat some of them as the speaker says them again!

Perhaps it is helpful to think of Deuteronomy as a piece of music as much as a piece of writing. It is like a fugue, the same motifs continually reappearing, perhaps in a different key but recognisably the same.

Another useful image is that of the hinge, as Deuteronomy is at a turning point in the Old Testament—the final book of the Pentateuch (the five books of the Law) and the first book of the Deuteronomic History, which runs from Joshua through to 2 Kings. As the name suggests, it is generally agreed that the same people were responsible for both Deuteronomy and the History, though there is no agreement as to who they were.

Deuteronomy itself is addressed to the people as they wait to enter the promised land, and can be divided into different sections. There is a core of law, from chapter 12 to 26, which many believe to be be the oldest part, perhaps going back to Moses and his period. There are two introductions—one from 4:44 to the end of chapter 11, which introduces this book, and a second from 1:1 to 4:43, which introduces the entire Deuteronomic History. Then there are the final chapters, which include the blessing of Moses for the tribes of Israel and his death. The final editing of the book probably took place during the exile, when the people were once again away from the land they had been promised. The writers constantly move between 'that day' of the past, 'this day' of the present and the future.

Throughout the book runs a clear message: remember God; remember what he has done for you and what you have promised in the covenant he has made with you. If you do this, all will go well for you. If you do not, there will be dire consequences, but God in his love is always willing to offer another chance.

*Helen Julian CSF*

DEUTERONOMY 1:1, 3, 7–8 (NRSV, ABRIDGED)

# Setting the scene

These are the words that Moses spoke to all Israel beyond the Jordan—in the wilderness, on the plain opposite Suph, between Paran and Tophel, Laban, Hazeroth, and Di-zahab... In the fortieth year, on the first day of the eleventh month, Moses spoke to the Israelites just as the Lord had commanded him to speak to them... 'Resume your journey... See, I have set the land before you; go in and take possession of the land that I swore to your ancestors, to Abraham, to Isaac, and to Jacob, to give to them and to their descendants after them.'

This is the start of the first of Deuteronomy's two introductions, which runs to 4:43. It is the one that sets the scene for the whole Deuteronomic History, so the writer is concerned to define the time and place clearly.

With all these place names, you would think it would be simple to pinpoint where Moses addressed the people, but some (Laban, Suph and Tophel) are unknown today and others are, in fact, scattered some distance apart. It is all quite confusing, but the most important 'place' is clear: the people are being addressed by Moses at the end of their 40 years in the wilderness, on the verge of entering the promised land.

Before they do that, Moses, as he does throughout this book, speaks God's word to them. Already, in these few verses, he introduces several of the themes that appear throughout the book, reminding God's people of their history so far and exhorting them to remain faithful to the God who has been faithful to them.

They are to go in and take possession of the land—also a key theme. One of God's promises to these wandering and homeless people was that they would be given a land of their own. Here, the covenant made by God with Abraham in Genesis 15 is about to be fulfilled, making promise another key theme. Also, Isaac and Jacob are included in that covenant, pointing to another theme of this book—ancestors.

So, the scene is set and we embark on the journey with the people.

## Reflection

*What are the main themes of your journey with God?*

HELEN JULIAN CSF

# Who is like our God?

For ask now about former ages, long before your own, ever since the day that God created human beings on the earth; ask from one end of heaven to the other: has anything so great as this ever happened or has its like ever been heard of? Has any people ever heard the voice of a god speaking out of a fire, as you have heard, and lived? Or has any god ever attempted to go and take a nation for himself from the midst of another nation, by trials, by signs and wonders, by war, by a mighty hand and an outstretched arm, and by terrifying displays of power, as the Lord your God did for you in Egypt before your very eyes?

In chapters 1—4, Moses has given the people a lightning tour of their history, from their escape from Egypt until their arrival at Horeb and the giving of the Ten Commandments.

Now he asks them to reflect on this story. Perhaps familiarity has bred if not contempt, at least a tendency to take it for granted. Moses urges the people to compare their story with the stories of the people around them. No other story in the whole history of the world since creation, from any nation anywhere, from one end of heaven to the other, will be as special as theirs.

It is a great piece of rhetoric. The succession of questions invite an audience response and we can imagine Moses pausing after each question for the crowd to shout their 'No!' We also have one of the often-repeated phrases that mark Deuteronomy: 'a mighty hand and an outstretched arm' (v. 34).

The uniqueness of Israel's God and the people he has chosen to be his own is another great theme in Deuteronomy. Here we can see the case for that uniqueness being built up by the appeal to history. This is history not simply as nostalgia but as a means of informing and shaping the people today and in the future.

### Prayer

*God of history, help me to look back, not to wallow in nostalgia but so as to be equipped and strengthened for today and tomorrow.*

HELEN JULIAN CSF

DEUTERONOMY 7:7–9 (NRSV)

# Chosen in love

It was not because you were more numerous than any other people that the Lord set his heart on you and chose you—for you were the fewest of all peoples. It was because the Lord loved you and kept the oath that he swore to your ancestors, that the Lord has brought you out with a mighty hand, and redeemed you from the house of slavery, from the hand of Pharaoh king of Egypt. Know therefore that the Lord your God is God, the faithful God who maintains covenant loyalty with those who love him and keep his commandments, to a thousand generations.

We all like to be special. From the child desperate to be chosen to answer the teacher's question to the elderly person delighted to be acknowledged by name, we want to feel that we are noticed and recognised. Trying too hard can be very offputting, however. We have probably all felt embarrassed on behalf of someone too desperate to be picked and many TV shows play on this desire in its positive and negative forms.

This passage is part of a section (7:1–11) that instructs the people about their future relationship with those already living in the land they will occupy. As part of that instruction they are reminded that God chose them not because they earned his favour or because they were the obvious choice—the biggest and best.

Instead, God chose them out of love and everything flowed from that. The promise to their ancestors, the exodus from Egypt, the giving of the Ten Commandments—everything that makes them God's people and shapes their lives—has been a gift freely given in love, by the God who is faithful. Peter makes a similar point writing to the Christian exiles: 'But you are a chosen race, a royal priesthood, a holy nation, God's own people... Once you were not a people, but now you are God's people' (1 Peter 2:9–10).

For the Israelites on the verge of entering the promised land, and the scattered exiles centuries later, the good news is that they are special, chosen and loved by God.

## Reflection

*How does it feel to be chosen, simply out of God's freely offered love?*

HELEN JULIAN CSF

# A very good land

For the Lord your God is bringing you into a good land, a land with flowing streams, with springs and underground waters welling up in valleys and hills, a land of wheat and barley, of vines and fig trees and pomegranates, a land of olive trees and honey, a land where you may eat bread without scarcity, where you will lack nothing, a land whose stones are iron and from whose hills you may mine copper. You shall eat your fill and bless the Lord your God for the good land that he has given you.

The land described here is almost a return to Eden, to paradise. Everything the people need will be given to them. After slavery in Egypt and then the long period of wandering in the desert, where sometimes the hardships of life made them long for Egypt again (Numbers 11:4–6), they are being given a fertile and beautiful land. These verses may well have originally been a self-contained hymn. 'Land' is mentioned six times and the first and last times it is referred to as 'good land'. The writer is taking no chances in getting his message across!

Two things are worth noticing. One is that they are given what is necessary and all that is necessary, but not more than that. They are not promised gold or silver, for example. Perhaps there is a lesson here, that we should be satisfied with 'enough'.

The second is that there is, in fact, no iron or copper west of the Jordan, so this is an idealised picture of the land, not a factual description of it.

In its wider context of the whole of chapter 8, the purpose of the passage becomes clear. Again, it is about remembering the past so as to shape behaviour in the future. Having a sufficiency, rather than prosperity, will not blunt the people's remembrance that it is God who has brought them here and given all these gifts. In later practice, each of the seven gifts—wheat, barley, vines and so on—was tithed at the festival of weeks (16:9–12). 'Do not forget God' is the constant message.

## Reflection

*How often do you thank God for his daily provision? If it is not every day, it is probably not often enough!*

HELEN JULIAN CSF

71

## Thursday 31 October
DEUTERONOMY 9:1, 4, 6 (NRSV)

# Difficult questions

Hear, O Israel! You are about to cross the Jordan today, to go in and dispossess nations larger and mightier than you, great cities, fortified to the heavens... When the Lord your God thrusts them out before you, do not say to yourself, 'It is because of my righteousness that the Lord has brought me in to occupy this land'; it is rather because of the wickedness of these nations that the Lord is dispossessing them before you... Know, then, that the Lord your God is not giving you this good land to occupy because of your righteousness, for you are a stubborn people.

The gift of the land has its darker side and here we confront it. The land that the Israelites entered was not empty. It was already occupied—but they were to dispossess these people and drive them out, or, rather, God was to accomplish this for them and with them.

The reality was that, in fact, the Canaanites were not driven out—the peoples coexisted—but this passage is one of those we can be tempted to skip over because it raises uncomfortable questions and forces us into the realms of present-day politics. We can see echoes of this passage and others like it in the whole apparently intractable recent history of Israel and Palestine, hinging ultimately on the question of who has the right to the land.

If we now go back to Deuteronomy and its times and writers, perhaps we can discern some unease there, too. Certainly the writer is trying to ensure that the Israelites do not think that they have earned the right to the land as a result of their own efforts. In a companion piece of theology to that which we saw in 7:7–9 on Tuesday (where the people are told that God chose them as an act of love, not because they deserved it), here the people are told, too, that the existing inhabitants are not being driven out because they, the Israelites, are so righteous. No, it is because of the wickedness of the Canaanites. Always it is God's initiative, which is, perhaps, one positive idea that we can take away from this thorny passage.

**Prayer**

*Pray for peace in Jerusalem.*

HELEN JULIAN CSF

# God's chosen place

These are the statutes and ordinances that you must diligently observe in the land that the Lord, the God of your ancestors, has given you to occupy all the days that you live on the earth. You must demolish completely all the places where the nations whom you are about to dispossess served their gods, on the mountain heights, on the hills, and under every leafy tree. Break down their altars, smash their pillars, burn their sacred poles with fire, and hew down the idols of their gods, and thus blot out their name from their places. You shall not worship the Lord your God in such ways. But you shall seek the place that the Lord your God will choose out of all your tribes as his habitation to put his name there.

This is the beginning of what is generally agreed to be the original core of Deuteronomy, chapters 12 to 26. These chapters may be the book that Hilkiah found in the temple, which sparked off Josiah's reform (2 Kings 22:8–13). Verse 1 sets the scene in characteristic fashion—reminding the people that the land is God's gift to them and this is the God of their ancestors.

This section consists almost entirely of laws, beginning with the laws about worship. First comes the command that the Israelites are not to take over the places of worship already in the land and, in fact, they are to destroy them utterly. In the Deuteronomic History, this becomes one of the key ways to evaluate kings (2 Kings 18:4, 23:14–15), which presumably means that it was an ongoing process rather than a once-for-all destruction.

The purpose of this destruction is to centralise worship in one place—which God will choose. In this one place, purity of worship of the one God could be ensured in a way that was not possible with shrines scattered all over the land. Jerusalem became this place, but is never named in Deuteronomy as the people have not yet entered the land, so this is still in the future.

### Reflection

*What are the gods and idols of our time and our land?*

HELEN JULIAN CSF

# God of the covenant

Moses convened all Israel, and said to them: Hear, O Israel, the statutes and ordinances that I am addressing to you today; you shall learn them and observe them diligently. The Lord our God made a covenant with us at Horeb. Not with our ancestors did the Lord make this covenant, but with us, who are all of us here alive today. The Lord spoke with you face to face at the mountain, out of the fire… And he said: I am the Lord your God, who brought you out of the land of Egypt, out of the house of slavery; you shall have no other gods before me.

The Law is another of the key themes of this book. Here Moses reminds the people how the Law was given originally, and goes on to repeat what is at the heart of the Law—the Ten Commandments. They come in this, the second introduction to the book, and chapters 5—11 form a kind of prologue to the more detailed working out of the Law in chapters 12—26.

There is something rather puzzling here. Moses says clearly, 'The Lord our God made a covenant with us at Horeb' (v. 2), but, according to 2:14, the generation of people who had taken part in the exodus and been present at the making of the covenant at Horeb all died out in the wilderness. So what is going on?

This is a good example of how history is never past for the writers of Deuteronomy: what happened once goes on being effective and important. The covenant at Horeb was made with 'all Israel', so Moses addresses 'all Israel' now. The covenant is as much for them and with them as it was for and with those who were actually present.

Christians have this same experience. The life and death and resurrection of Jesus are as important for us now as they were for those who witnessed them first hand.

God still says to the Israelites, 'I am', just as God still speaks to us, in a covenant of intimacy and of love, but one that also makes demands.

### Prayer

*Lord of the eternal covenant, let me hear you speaking today as you have always spoken to your people.*

HELEN JULIAN CSF

# Hear, O Israel

Now this is the commandment—the statutes and the ordinances—that the Lord your God charged me to teach you to observe in the land that you are about to cross into and occupy, so that you and your children and your children's children, may fear the Lord your God all the days of your life, and keep all his decrees and his commandments that I am commanding you, so that your days may be long... Hear, O Israel: The Lord is our God, the Lord alone. You shall love the Lord your God with all your heart, and with all your soul, and with all your might.

You may be noticing that there is a lot of repetition in Deuteronomy. If we are told to keep the statutes and ordinances once, we are told dozens of times. It is one of the features of a book meant to teach. As teachers all know, you need to repeat the key elements of the teaching many times to be sure they are being heard.

It is also necessary to find striking and memorable summaries, however, and the final section of today's passage is one of those. Beginning 'Hear, O Israel' (v. 4), it is known as the Shema, from the Hebrew for those words, and has become the principal Jewish confession of faith. Jesus would have known it well and, indeed, he quoted it as the 'greatest and first commandment' (Matthew 22:36–38).

'The Lord is our God, the Lord alone' (v. 4) is ambiguous in the Hebrew: it can be an assertion of monotheism (there is only one God) or stress oneness (the same God is worshipped wherever worship is offered) or affirm that only Israel's God is to be worshipped as Lord. Perhaps all are intended; certainly all these meanings give a depth to the phrase.

Heart and soul and might (Jesus changes this last to 'mind' in Matthew 22:37) can be seen as three parts of human nature and, hence, can be a call to love and serve God with all of ourselves. Our faith is not to be just a matter of the emotions or of the mind or of our actions, but of all that we are.

### Reflection

*What is your personal Shema—your one-sentence confession of faith?*

HELEN JULIAN CSF

DEUTERONOMY 11:18–21 (NRSV)

# Loving the word

You shall put these words of mine in your heart and soul, and you shall bind them as a sign on your hand, and fix them as an emblem on your forehead. Teach them to your children, talking about them when you are at home and when you are away, when you lie down and when you rise. Write them on the doorposts of your house and on your gates, so that your days and the days of your children may be multiplied in the land that the Lord swore to your ancestors to give them, as long as the heavens are above the earth.

For its original Jewish hearers, this passage (and the very similar one at 6:6–9) gave rise over time to two physical ways of obeying it. Jewish men wore phylacteries (Matthew 23:5 has a not very flattering reference to them), which were small boxes containing key texts with thongs to fasten them to the forehead and the left forearm. Also, a mezuzah was fastened to the right-hand doorpost of houses. This is a small container, again containing key texts, to be touched as you enter or leave the house. The chosen texts were two from Deuteronomy (6:4–9 and 11:13–21) and Exodus 13:1–16.

To me, these speak of the importance of putting our faith into practice. Each faith will find its own ways and Christians are not necessarily called to copy the ways of their Jewish brothers and sisters.

This passage is an encouragement to fall in love with God's words, to be, in a positive way, obsessed with them, as someone newly in love is obsessed with the one they love. Out of this passion, we will find ways to include them in all aspects of our lives and allow them to shape all those aspects. They are to be in our inner spiritual lives and seen in us by those around us. They are to be central in our families and our lives outside the home. They are to be our first thought on rising and our last thought on sleeping. They are to mark the boundaries of our homes and, implicitly, our lives.

## Reflection

*How do you live out your love of God's word?*

HELEN JULIAN CSF

# Radical generosity

If there is among you anyone in need, a member of your community in any of your towns within the land that the Lord your God is giving you, do not be hard-hearted or tight-fisted towards your needy neighbour. You should rather open your hand, willingly lending enough to meet the need, whatever it may be. Be careful that you do not entertain a mean thought, thinking, 'The seventh year, the year of remission, is near', and therefore view your needy neighbour with hostility and give nothing; your neighbour might cry to the Lord against you, and you would incur guilt.

We have moved back into the core of the book, the Law that defines how Israel is to live in the promised land. This is one of the more radical parts. It is worth reading the whole passage, of which the above is part: 15:1–11. Verses 1–2 are the Law, verses 3–11 teaching how to apply it.

If you read the whole passage, you will notice what appears to be a contradiction. In verse 4, 'there will be no one in need among you', while in verse 11 we have, 'there will never cease to be some in need on the earth'. This seems to be a recognition of the ideal and the reality. If the people were able to keep the Law entirely and completely, then there would, indeed, be no one in need. They will inevitably fail in this task, however, so provision has to be made for the poor so that they do not remain forever in poverty.

Every seven years there is a fresh start, all debts being written off. You may remember the Jubilee 2000 campaign leading up to the millennium. It was an international application of this ideal, campaigning for heavily indebted poor countries to be forgiven their debts.

It sparked off some of the same human reactions that the writer mentions here—that the lenders might be reluctant to lend if they know the debt might be wiped out before it has been repaid. God's command is to be generous, however: he has given the land to the people, so they are to share its wealth.

### Reflection

*How do you share what God has given you?*

Helen Julian CSF

# Choose life

See, I have set before you today life and prosperity, death and adversity. If you obey the commandments of the Lord your God... then you shall live and become numerous, and the Lord your God will bless you in the land that you are entering to possess. But if your heart turns away and you do not hear, but are led astray to bow down to other gods and serve them, I declare to you today that you shall perish; you shall not live long in the land that you are crossing the Jordan to enter and possess. I call heaven and earth to witness against you today that I have set before you life and death, blessings and curses. Choose life so that you and your descendants may live.

Now we move on to the chapters added to the end of the book, usually identified as Moses' final address. In one way this is yet another repetition of the core message of the whole book: keep the commandments and you will prosper; fail to keep them and disaster will be the result.

This is, however, a particularly striking picture of the choice that is before the people then and before each one of us today. Moses crystallises many chapters of pleas, rules, promises and threats into one basic challenge: who will you serve?

The form of this challenge is reminiscent of the way covenants between nations were worded in this period and that part of the world. This part of the book may well have been used in covenant-making and covenant renewal ceremonies between Israel and their God. They normally included a reminder of the history of the nations, a statement of general principles, the detailed obligations of the agreement and the consequences of keeping or not keeping it. So, here we are in the final section, with the choice of life and prosperity, death and adversity starkly spelled out. The witnesses to the covenant are heaven and earth—the whole created order.

Notice, though, that God does not compel obedience; in the end the call to the people—as it is to us—is to 'choose life' (v. 19).

**Prayer**

*Lord, help me today and every day to choose life.*

HELEN JULIAN CSF

# God of second chances

When all these things have happened to you, the blessings and the curses that I have set before you, if you call them to mind among all the nations where the Lord your God has driven you, and return to the Lord your God, and you and your children obey him with all your heart and with all your soul, just as I am commanding you today, then the Lord your God will restore your fortunes and have compassion on you, gathering you again from all the peoples among whom the Lord your God has scattered you. Even if you are exiled to the ends of the world, from there the Lord your God will gather you, and from there he will bring you back.

This passage reflects starkly the situation at the time when Deuteronomy was undergoing its final revisions and editing, so was therefore probably added then. The people had failed to keep the covenant and the curses and adversity had come down on them. They had been conquered and taken out of the land that God had given them, into exile. They could no longer worship in Jerusalem. The whole theological basis of their life had collapsed. They must have felt hopeless, bewildered and tempted to abandon their previous faith.

The writer seeks to give them hope nonetheless. At the beginning of the book, the people stood outside the land, ready to enter it. Now, they are once again outside the land and God can again rescue them as he did in the exodus from Egypt, bringing them back to the land

The conditions are the same as before: remember what God has done and commanded, and be ready, even now, to turn back. The word translated 'return' can also mean 'be converted'. It does not matter how far they have strayed. Even from 'the ends of the world' (v. 4) God can and will gather them and bring them back.

God never gives up and is always willing to offer another chance. The door is always open for his people to return to him.

## Reflection

*Is there any part of your life that means you need to return, to be once again converted to God's ways?*

HELEN JULIAN CSF

# Applying the Law

When someone is convicted of a crime punishable by death and is executed, and you hang him on a tree, his corpse must not remain all night upon the tree; you shall bury him that same day, for anyone hung on a tree is under God's curse. You must not defile the land that the Lord your God is giving you for possession... If you come on a bird's nest... with the mother sitting on the fledglings or on the eggs, you shall not take the mother with the young. Let the mother go, taking only the young for yourself... You shall not wear clothes made of wool and linen woven together.

The Law in the core part of this book varies enormously in its subject matter and relevance to us today. Some of it, for example, supposes a sacrificial system of worship that we no longer follow or an acceptance of slavery.

There are other parts that remain valuable, however. Deuteronomy is one of the Old Testament books quoted most often in the New Testament and, indeed, the first part of today's reading is used by Paul in the letter to the Galatians (3:13). He puts it into a Christian context, in a section on the Law and faith, showing how Jesus redeems us from the curse of being unable to keep the entire Law by becoming himself a curse in the crucifixion. As an innocent victim, he did away with the curse and opened the way for everyone to share in the blessing of Abraham and the new covenant.

Though not the meaning the original writer intended, it is a creative reusing of the tradition in the new circumstances of the new covenant.

The second point of the Law covered in today's passage is one that may have new significance for our time as we commit to using the earth's resources sustainably. We are not just to think for today and our own needs but also leave the 'mother bird' so that she can go on to produce in the future.

The final point probably reflects Israel's concern for purity in life and worship.

## Reflection

*How do we discern what parts of past inspiration are still relevant today?*

HELEN JULIAN CSF

DEUTERONOMY 26:2–7 (NRSV, ABRIDGED)

# We were there

You shall take some of the fruit of the ground... and you shall put it in a basket and go to the place that the Lord your God will choose as a dwelling for his name... When the priest takes the basket from your hand and sets it down before the altar of the Lord your God, you shall make this response... 'A wandering Aramean was my ancestor; he went down into Egypt and lived there as an alien, few in number, and there he became a great nation, mighty and populous. When the Egyptians treated us harshly and afflicted us, by imposing hard labour on us, we cried to the Lord, the God of our ancestors.'

The stories we tell are an important part of our identity. When we gather as families or as church communities, the stories we share with one another remind us of our history with one another and of what is important in our past.

This story is told in the context of worship, perhaps as part of the Feast of Weeks or at Passover. Again, we see the importance of worshipping at the place God will choose and acknowledging that the land is God's gift by giving back to God some of what it produces. The 'wandering Aramean' is Jacob, whose mother Rebecca was from Aram-naharaim in Mesopotamia (Genesis 24:10). Note that the word 'wandering' is a strong one: it could also mean 'homeless' or even 'doomed to perish'.

One of the fascinating things about this passage is how the pronouns change. Initially the story is told about 'he', then suddenly it becomes 'our' story: 'When the Egyptians treated *us* harshly' (v. 6). It is a wonderful example of how history is not just about what happened to other people. If we identify ourselves with a group, a nation, a church, what happened to them in the past happened to us also because it shaped our present identity.

The pattern of oppression, cry for help, and God's action in response is a very characteristic one for this book, completing a passage that is rich in key themes and worth reading in its entirety.

### Reflection
*What important stories do you tell and retell?*

HELEN JULIAN CSF

# Remember

> When the Lord your God has brought you into the land that he
> swore to your ancestors, to Abraham, to Isaac, and to Jacob, to
> give you—a land with fine, large cities that you did not build,
> houses filled with all sorts of goods that you did not fill, hewn
> cisterns that you did not hew, vineyards and olive groves that you
> did not plant—and when you have eaten your fill, take care that
> you do not forget the Lord, who brought you out of the land of
> Egypt, out of the house of slavery.

As we come to the end of our journey through Deuteronomy, this passage recaps many of its themes. That in itself is a theme as there is a lot of repetition of the important ideas in this book. It can make it difficult to read, but recognising the themes as they come round can help, along with being aware that its primary purpose is to teach and warn.

The list of gifts (see also Joshua 24:13) is generally acknowledged to come from an ancient blessing. The corresponding curse can be found at 28:16, 30b and in Amos 5:11. God fulfilled his promises, bringing the people into a land of bounty and giving them everything they needed. These promises sustained them throughout their wandering in the wilderness, but it is a human tendency to remember plans and promises better when they are still unfulfilled. They provide motivation to keep moving, keep working. Once the promise has been fulfilled and the plan put into practice, however, it was easy for the people to sit back, drift and believe that they had done it all by themselves. In this final passage, therefore, they are reminded that it is God who brought them into the land, as he promised.

They are also reminded that he had brought them out of a land—out of the land of Egypt, out of slavery. They owe God their liberty as well as their livelihood. As we keep Remembrance Sunday, we give thanks to God for all his gifts and recall those who gave their lives in order to preserve our liberty as God did that of his people.

### Prayer

*God of freedom, let us never take our freedom for granted.*

HELEN JULIAN CSF

# After Pentecost: Acts 21—24

Acts 21—24 tells the story of Paul's travels around the Mediterranean basin, particularly his visit to Jerusalem that almost ended in disaster for him. Recognised ministers in several communities had warned him not to make the journey to Jerusalem, but he went anyway and narrowly escaped with his life.

From a theological point of view, Paul's risk-taking gives us some clues as to the author's theological ideal of what the calling and attributes of an apostle are all about. Paul, like Stephen, had a prophetic ministry and was willing, like Christ, to become a martyr if necessary. Taken simply as an account of human behaviour, however, it is just as possible to read the story as evidence that Paul was so single-minded that he refused to listen to those around him and got out of trouble using his own human wiles, which is not usually a trait that would draw much admiration or affection for a minister. Yet, the story is narrated in such a way as to exonerate Paul, suggesting that he had a clear grasp of his calling and a deep and abiding trust in the power of God. He did not simply trust in God's power to get him out of trouble, but was even prepared to die if that was the cost of preaching the gospel.

This section towards the end of the Acts of the Apostles, then, not only gives us further episodes from Paul's adventures but also offers us the chance to reflect on the theology of ministry, the relationship between our personal convictions and abilities and the guiding and empowering role of the Holy Spirit. When should we take advice? When should we follow what we sense to be our hearts' longing? If we capitalise on our human wiles, should we attribute the outcome to the Holy Spirit? Paul seems anything but sensible, but, to the extent that the story translates across the centuries, how much does it reveal the weaknesses of this charismatic religious leader and how much does it challenge us to take more risks?

As we begin our series of passages, let us pray: 'Lord God, thank you for your servant Paul. May we understand a little more of his passion for you and, in so doing, find our own passion for you renewed.'

*Maggi Dawn*

ACTS 21:1–3 (NRSV)

# Eyewitness

When we had parted from them and set sail, we came by a straight course to Cos, and the next day to Rhodes, and from there to Patara. When we found a ship bound for Phoenicia, we went on board and set sail. We came in sight of Cyprus; and leaving it on our left, we sailed to Syria and landed at Tyre, because the ship was to unload its cargo there.

The Acts of the Apostles begins with Jesus' ascension and Pentecost (Acts 1—2), then continues with Paul witnessing the death of Stephen, the first martyr (7:54–60; 22:20). Much of the book then recounts the stories of Paul's journeys as he took the gospel all over the Gentile world.

Scholars have often wondered who wrote Acts. Passages such as this one, where the narrator uses the first person plural, are known as the 'we' passages and have been taken as evidence that the narrator was an eyewitness to events, thus giving Acts historical credibility. Because Luke is believed to be the author, the assumption is that he is referring to himself here. In fact, however, the author never reveals his identity and never claims to have been present. So it is just as possible that the author created this first-person construct for a different reason. One theory, for instance, is that Luke wrote Acts but wrote it from the point of view of Barnabas.

Whatever the truth might be, these 'we' passages do connect the whole story together with the sense that this is not just a tale to be told but a story that draws the reader into its significance. Indeed, whenever theology is written in the first person, it engages the reader in a personal way, giving the sense that it is not only about history or doctrine but experience, too. We can understand a great deal about the theory of Christianity without ever 'getting' what it is about on a personal level. To understand the whole picture, however, the reader has to climb inside the story, as it were, and own it, not just in an imaginary world but also in the first person and in the present tense.

### Prayer
*Dear Lord, where do I fit in this story?*

MAGGI DAWN

# Warnings

We looked up the disciples and stayed there for seven days. Through the Spirit they told Paul not to go on to Jerusalem. When our days there were ended, we left and proceeded on our journey; and all of them, with wives and children, escorted us outside the city. There we knelt down on the beach and prayed and said farewell to one another. Then we went on board the ship, and they returned home... While we were staying [in Tyre] for several days, a prophet named Agabus came down from Judea. He came to us and took Paul's belt, bound his own feet and hands with it, and said, 'Thus says the Holy Spirit, "This is the way the Jews in Jerusalem will bind the man who owns this belt and will hand him over to the Gentiles."'

When their cargo ship landed at Tyre, Paul's team had an enforced lay-over. Travel was less direct and simple in the ancient world than it is today, but, instead of getting stressed, Paul simply used the time to catch up with local Christians. Perhaps he was just more reconciled to slow travel than we are. How often do we fixate on the destination, only to miss the experiences we might have along the way?

Although he is renowned as an evangelist, wherever Paul went his first priority was to encourage and build up the church. Today's world tends to insist on specialisation: are you an evangelist, a pastor or a preacher? Paul's life suggests that ministry is not quite so neatly divided up—that people may have various combinations of gifts, and a call to mission does not preclude a concern for pastoral work with the congregation.

At Tyre, the local Christians discern danger in Paul's proposed journey and warn him not to go (v. 4). Later, Paul receives another warning from Agabus the prophet, who uses symbolic action somewhat reminiscent of an Old Testament prophet such as Jeremiah to tell Paul again, urgently, that Jerusalem carries grave danger for him. It seems that the Holy Spirit is strongly leading Paul to abandon his trip, but will Paul listen?

### Prayer
*Lord, am I listening? Are you speaking to me through others?*

MAGGI DAWN

# Advice unheeded

When we heard this, we and the people there urged [Paul] not to go up to Jerusalem. Then Paul answered, 'What are you doing, weeping and breaking my heart? For I am ready not only to be bound but even to die in Jerusalem for the name of the Lord Jesus.' Since he would not be persuaded, we remained silent except to say, 'The Lord's will be done.'

Paul's friends as well as the local people begged him not to go to Jerusalem, yet Paul 'would not be persuaded' (v. 14). The response from Paul's team to his reaction to their fears suggests that they knew there was no point in arguing with him if his mind was made up.

Was Paul right to ignore the advice of both strangers and friends? Even Jesus rejected the urging of his disciples to avoid danger because his own prophetic calling could not be fulfilled if he fled from danger. Similarly, one of the author's overarching threads in Acts is the unfolding picture of Paul as a prophet-martyr in the same mould as Christ himself. Hence, regardless of warnings about danger, he is determined to continue with his mission. The difference, though, is that while Jesus seemed to know God's will and the disciples did not, Paul is here apparently rejecting divine guidance.

From a purely human point of view, Acts can also be read as a demonstration that the apostles were full of idiosyncrasies, spreading the gospel not only through their brilliant, God-inspired actions, but also despite their weaknesses and mistakes. Paul, like many a charismatic leader, was stubbornly single-minded. Perhaps he should have listened to his friends rather than putting them, as well as himself, in danger.

A leader who ignores the counsel of others is today usually considered irresponsible. Then, while Paul's friends knew there was no point in arguing with him, they did not abandon him to his mission. Perhaps they realised that his gifts made it worth putting up with his weaknesses and recognised, too, that he needed them.

### Prayer

*God, teach me to listen to you, to others and to my own heart and be a faithful friend even to people who do not listen.*

MAGGI DAWN

# Disagreeing and loving

When we arrived in Jerusalem, the brothers welcomed us warmly. The next day Paul went with us to visit James; and all the elders were present. After greeting them, he related one by one the things that God had done among the Gentiles through his ministry. When they heard it, they praised God. Then they said to him, 'You see, brother, how many thousands of believers there are among the Jews, and they are all zealous for the law. They have been told about you that you teach all the Jews living among the Gentiles to forsake Moses, and that you tell them not to circumcise their children or observe the customs. What then is to be done?'

Paul's Jerusalem colleagues celebrated his arrival and the accounts of his travels, but soon they explained why his visit put him at risk. Thousands of Christians living in Jerusalem had heard the rumour that Paul was teaching Jewish Christians living further afield to abandon their traditional customs. Only a few years earlier, the Jerusalem crowds had turned on Jesus. Now Paul was at risk, from both the Roman authorities and the company of Jewish Christians whose passion for their faith could be the undoing of Paul.

It is one of the oddities of passionate religious commitment that faith in a God of love and justice can lead people to act in unjust and unloving ways, but religious impulses quickly become political. This is partly because true faith affects every part of life and partly because if faith matters at all, it matters completely. A view of faith that seems to cheapen our own is hard to tolerate.

At the same time, we should note that the elders to whom Paul turned had resolved a similar disagreement with him earlier. Acts 15 relates his argument with Peter and how the two sides reconciled themselves, recognising that different views on certain issues did not necessarily threaten the integrity of either side. It really is possible for people with significantly different views to coexist peacefully within the church.

### Prayer

*Help us, Lord, never to let our commitment to truth overrule a passionate commitment to love others, even when we do not see eye to eye with them.*

MAGGI DAWN

# Freedom and faithfulness

[The elders said] 'So do what we tell you. We have four men who are under a vow. Join these men, go through the rite of purification with them, and pay for the shaving of their heads. Thus all will know that there is nothing in what they have been told about you, but that you yourself observe and guard the law. But as for the Gentiles who have become believers, we have sent a letter with our judgement that they should abstain from what has been sacrificed to idols and from blood and from what is strangled and from fornication.' Then Paul took the men, and the next day, having purified himself, he entered the temple with them, making public the completion of the days of purification when the sacrifice would be made for each of them.

The elders advised Paul to demonstrate publicly his faithfulness to his Jewish background. The four men had, like Paul himself, taken a Nazirite vow, which included not cutting their hair. When the period of the vow came to an end, a ritual had to be observed (Numbers 6:18), which began with having the dedicated hair shaved off and burned. Paul had done this earlier (Acts 18:18) and, by repeating the ritual with four other Nazirites, he would be making a public demonstration of his obedience to Mosaic Law. The elders hoped this would stave off rumours of Paul's apostasy.

Paul had consistently argued that Gentiles did not need to adopt Jewish customs in order to be Christians, but this action was consistent with his teaching. Although he no longer considered himself bound by Jewish Law because of his freedom in Christ, he happily kept the Law in order to maintain his relationships with fellow Jewish Christians (1 Corinthians 9:20). His point is that freedom in Christ does not demand cultural conformity, as it is not cultural rituals that procure our salvation. This means that believers are free to take part in them, as long as they do not involve worshipping false gods or cause other Christians to doubt their own faith. Consequently, many kinds of cultural difference can stand side by side within Christianity.

### Prayer

*Lord, help us to celebrate different cultural expressions of faith without feeling threatened.*

Maggi Dawn

# Dealing with difference

When the seven days were almost completed, the Jews from Asia, who had seen him in the temple, stirred up the whole crowd. They seized him, shouting, 'Fellow-Israelites, help! This is the man who is teaching everyone everywhere against our people, our law, and this place; more than that, he has actually brought Greeks into the temple and has defiled this holy place.' For they had previously seen Trophimus the Ephesian with him in the city, and they supposed that Paul had brought him into the temple.

Jesus was roundly criticised for socialising with the wrong types of people (Luke 15:1–2)—in this case seemingly because his association with them made him ritually unclean. In Paul's case, some of his critics saw him with a Gentile, others saw him in the temple and several had heard rumours of his teaching, all of which added up to a picture of a man who was treating hallowed customs with wilful disrespect.

How easy it is to regard people as being 'guilty by association' and how dangerous it is to add half-truths together and make assumptions. It is not that it is wrong to ask questions—it should always be right to ask questions—but 'stirring up the crowd' is quite another thing. It may seem like mere petty gossip on one level, yet so many of history's atrocities have been perpetrated on the back of just this kind of rumour and misinformation. Genocides, holocausts, racial segregation—the list goes on.

Once again, Acts raises the thorny issue of human difference: how do we live side by side with people whose beliefs and customs are different from our own? It is often easier to accept dramatic difference than subtle variations on our own treasured beliefs or practices. Loving and accepting others means giving them the benefit of the doubt, listening closely to their own stories and not rushing to assume that we understand their motives simply on the basis of surface details.

**Prayer**
*Lord, help us to be open to people who are not like us.*

MAGGI DAWN

Acts 21:30–36 (NRSV, abridged)

# Prophet and martyr

Then all the city was aroused, and the people rushed together. They seized Paul and dragged him out of the temple, and immediately the doors were shut. While they were trying to kill him, word came to the tribune of the cohort that all Jerusalem was in an uproar. Immediately he took soldiers and centurions and ran down to them… Then the tribune came, arrested [Paul], and ordered him to be bound with two chains; he inquired who he was and what he had done. Some in the crowd shouted one thing, some another; and… When Paul came to the steps, the violence of the mob was so great that he had to be carried by the soldiers. The crowd that followed kept shouting, 'Away with him!'

Acts gives us glimpses of Paul as a brilliant but stubborn leader, ignoring warnings from the Holy Spirit and his friends. This chimes with our own experiences as it is not unusual to be caught between opposing opinions, each of which lays claim to being the guidance of the Holy Spirit.

The story as Luke tells it, though, is woven around two central themes. The primary theme—Pentecost and the theology of the Holy Spirit—is introduced at the very beginning of the book, then continues as a tale of how the Spirit guides and grows the Church.

The second theme is introduced as Paul (then called Saul) witnessed the martyrdom of Stephen, who gave the most concise and complete account of the gospel just before he died (Acts 7). Stephen spoke prophetically of Jesus as prophet and martyr, then mirrored his own message in his death. Saul supported Stephen's executioners, but he never forgot that moment and, subsequently, took on the mantle of prophet and martyr himself.

This suggests a theological interpretation of Paul's seemingly reckless disregard for the warnings that now came through the Spirit. Taken in the context of the central theme of Christ and his followers as prophet-martyrs, a warning of martyrdom is not a reason to run in the opposite direction but, rather, to take the prophetic opportunity, even if it might result in death.

### Prayer
*Help us, O God, to be courageous prophets of truth.*

Maggi Dawn

# Learning and faith

Just as Paul was about to be brought into the barracks, he said to the tribune, 'May I say something to you?' The tribune replied, 'Do you know Greek? Then you are not the Egyptian who recently stirred up a revolt and led the four thousand assassins out into the wilderness?' Paul replied, 'I am a Jew, from Tarsus in Cilicia, a citizen of an important city; I beg you, let me speak to the people.' When he had given him permission, Paul stood on the steps and motioned to the people for silence; and when there was a great hush, he addressed them in the Hebrew language.

One of the challenges thrown at academic theologians is that all their learning has nothing to do with real faith. I have even heard students at Cambridge and Yale say this, emerging from their own theological studies. Advanced study is surely not a prerequisite for faith, but we should not assume that academic theology is opposed to 'real' faith. It certainly saved Paul's skin in this situation: his learning, extensive travels and inquisitive mind meant that he had acquired a degree of sophistication in understanding other people as well as himself. His legal training, his ability to speak several languages and his multicultural vision enabled him to speak, literally, across cultural, racial and political boundaries.

In the moment of crisis, then, while Paul's journey was clearly attributed to divine inspiration, the Holy Spirit also worked through his own abilities. There is something satisfying about seeing this confluence of human and spiritual gifting, the risk-taker depending on the Spirit, yet still employing every ounce of his own abilities to carry out his work.

Inspiration literally means being 'in-spirited', breathed into, given breath. Indeed, some extreme theologies of the Holy Spirit suggest that the Spirit takes over humans, speaking through them as if they are nothing more than a mouthpiece possessed by God. The story of the early church suggests a far more interactive theology—a relationship between a person and God, an interaction between natural and supernatural, a range of human achievements brought to life by the breath of God.

### Prayer
*Help me develop all my gifts in your service, Lord.*

MAGGI DAWN

# Wise mentor

When [the crowd] heard [Paul] addressing them in Hebrew, they became even more quiet. Then he said: 'I am a Jew, born in Tarsus in Cilicia, but brought up in this city at the feet of Gamaliel, educated strictly according to our ancestral law, being zealous for God, just as all of you are today. I persecuted this Way up to the point of death by binding both men and women and putting them in prison, as the high priest and the whole council of elders can testify about me. From them I also received letters to the brothers in Damascus, and I went there in order to bind those who were there and to bring them back to Jerusalem for punishment.'

Paul's insistence that acceptance under the broad umbrella of the gospel did not require cultural conformity makes him sound like the first ecumenical minister. How did he arrive at this broad-minded approach? There may be a clue in his mentor, Gamaliel (v. 3): 'a Pharisee… a teacher of the law, respected by all the people' (5:34).

When Gamaliel first appeared in Acts 5, he made a judgment about the emergence of the early church as it began as a sect within Judaism. Then, too, an enraged crowd wanted to kill the Christians who (it seemed to the crowd) were perverting their own tradition. Gamaliel, however, called for calm and put it to the crowd that killing on the basis of religious conviction served no purpose: 'Let them alone,' he advised, 'because if this plan… is of human origin, it will fail; but if it is of God, you will not be able to overthrow them—in that case you may even be found fighting against God!' (vv. 38–39). Gamaliel's calm wisdom was to let differences of interpretation alone and let God take care of it.

We have no record of how Paul's attitudes were shaped by his mentor, but it is reasonable to suppose that Gamaliel's wisdom had some impact on him when he faced the uncharted waters of including Gentile culture and practice within Christianity.

**Prayer**

*Lord, give us wisdom and patience, that we might not be found fighting against your purposes.*

MAGGI DAWN

# Defending God?

'While I was... approaching Damascus, about noon a great light from heaven suddenly shone about me. I fell to the ground and heard a voice saying to me, "Saul, Saul, why are you persecuting me?" I answered, "Who are you, Lord?" Then he said to me, "I am Jesus of Nazareth whom you are persecuting." Now those who were with me saw the light but did not hear the voice... speaking to me. I asked, "What am I to do, Lord?" The Lord said to me, "Get up and go to Damascus; there you will be told everything that has been assigned to you to do." Since I could not see because of the brightness of that light, those who were with me took my hand and led me to Damascus.'

The irony of this passage (and of yesterday's) is that Paul, who spent his early career throwing others in jail, now faces the possibility of being incarcerated himself. The dramatic thrust of this famous passage about Paul's experience on the Damascus road, however, is that by persecuting Christians, he was, in reality, persecuting the very God he thought he was protecting. What are the lessons here?

The first, perhaps, is to remember that we are not required to look after God's reputation. We do not need to defend or protect God against other people, as if God were weak and helpless without us.

The second is perhaps even more important. It is that, in the words of Jesus, 'just as you did it to one of the least of these who are members of my family, you did it to me' (Matthew 25:40). The fourth-century theologian Athanasius drew attention to the idea that, because people are made in the image of God, in some sense God resides in each person. The Hindu practice of 'namaste' echoes this idea as two people meeting bow towards each other with their hands together, meaning that God, who resides in me, greets God who also resides in you. Although these faiths are different, the ideas of each are similar: that is, if we persecute and abuse others, we persecute God; if we bless and care for others, we bless God.

### Prayer

*Lord, help me see your image in everyone I meet.*

MAGGI DAWN

# Grace and redemption

'Ananias, who was a devout man according to the law and well spoken of by all the Jews living there, came to me... Then he said, "The God of our ancestors has chosen you... you will be his witness to all the world of what you have seen and heard... Get up, be baptised, and have your sins washed away, calling on his name." After I had returned to Jerusalem and while I was praying in the temple, I fell into a trance and saw Jesus saying to me, "Hurry and get out of Jerusalem quickly, because they will not accept your testimony about me." And I said, "Lord, they themselves know that in every synagogue I imprisoned and beat those who believed in you. And while the blood of your witness Stephen was shed, I myself was standing by, approving and keeping the coats of those who killed him." Then he said to me, "Go, for I will send you far away to the Gentiles."'

Paul's second vision of Jesus occurred in the temple for, like almost all those who followed Jesus at this time, Paul still counted himself a faithful and observant Jew. We also see here some suggestion as to why he became a missionary to the Gentiles. Once he became a worshipper of Jesus, his days as a campaigner against 'the Way' (the name for the fledgling sect of Christ-followers) were over, but Paul realised that, having so cruelly abused them, he would not find a home among them in the near future. There is, perhaps, some sense of creative redemption in the fact that it was precisely Paul's persecution of them that made it necessary for him to travel far away and, in turn, this led to him becoming the apostle to the Gentiles.

That said, it would be a travesty of the gospel to suggest that cruelty is justified by a later, good outcome. Redemption does not imply paying back or making good, however. It suggests bringing something good, unexpectedly, from completely unpromising circumstances. Redemption is pure grace, not payback.

### Prayer

*Lord, when we have failed, let us remember that grace may still lead to the hope of redemption.*

MAGGI DAWN

# Privileged

Then [the crowd] shouted, 'Away with such a fellow from the earth! For he should not be allowed to live.' And while they were shouting, throwing off their cloaks, and tossing dust into the air, the tribune directed that he was to be brought into the barracks, and ordered him to be examined by flogging, to find out the reason for this outcry against him. But when they had tied him up with thongs, Paul said to the centurion who was standing by, 'Is it legal for you to flog a Roman citizen who is uncondemned?'... The tribune came and asked Paul, 'Tell me, are you a Roman citizen?' And he said, 'Yes.'... Immediately those who were about to examine him drew back from him; and the tribune also was afraid, for he realised that Paul was a Roman citizen and that he had bound him.

Because of the power of the Roman empire, it was said that a Roman citizen could walk from one end of the world to the other safe and unchallenged; no one would dare lay a finger on them for fear of the consequences. Paul was a Roman citizen—not by wealth or merit, but by birth (v. 28).

Paul was once miraculously released from prison and later had a vision of Jesus to sustain him when he was arrested (23:11). Here, though, his escape from danger rests not on divine intervention but on human privilege. That does not necessarily sit comfortably with Christian ideals, as getting ahead based on privilege does not seem to stack up with Jesus' teachings about the poor or about being willing to serve and wash the feet of others.

Paul, though, seems to have no qualms about drawing on every means available to him to get the job done, whether by prayer and miracles, gifts and abilities or, in this case, the privilege of birth and background. Is it possible that we can sometimes be so fixed on supernatural guidance that we dismiss our ordinary skills and everyday gifts? There is a place for simply using everything at our disposal in the service of God.

## Prayer

*Lord, make me wise, to know when to wait for you and when to use human resources to pursue my calling.*

MAGGI DAWN

# A true apostle

Then a great clamour arose, and certain scribes of the Pharisees' group stood up and contended, 'We find nothing wrong with this man. What if a spirit or an angel has spoken to him?' When the dissension became violent, the tribune, fearing that they would tear Paul to pieces, ordered the soldiers to go down, take him by force, and bring him into the barracks. That night the Lord stood near him and said, 'Keep up your courage! For just as you have testified for me in Jerusalem, so you must bear witness also in Rome.'

Again, we see here the idea of the prophet and martyr. Paul speaks and the people hear echoes of God in his words, but every time it puts him in danger. The Lord speaks directly to Paul, affirming that he is called to preach the gospel despite the consequences. Paul, it seems, is exonerated from the charge of being stubborn or not listening to his team earlier in the story. The danger is real, but it is a consequence of preaching the gospel. Having survived in Jerusalem, the scene is now set for him to continue on to Rome.

Paul's claim to being an apostle is indicated in this reading and elsewhere. All the apostles except Paul had known Jesus personally while he was alive, but Paul had this series of visions in which he seemed to 'meet' Jesus and this direct revelation, he claimed, was what qualified him to be an apostle.

Rome, like Jerusalem, would be a place that demanded the prophet-martyr role from Paul. Christ's words (v. 11) proved prophetic, for Paul did end up preaching in Rome, where he was eventually imprisoned before his death. 'Keep up your courage' (v. 11), though, gives the whole endeavour a human aspect. Paul sometimes seems to be superhuman in his exploits and determination, but here we see Christ tenderly encouraging him, knowing that without divine help Paul could not sustain the energy and commitment required to carry out his apostolic charge.

### Prayer

*Lord, help me to hear your voice of encouragement. Help me to be courageous and tenacious, never letting go of the knowledge that I am called by you.*

MAGGI DAWN

ACTS 24:22–27 (NRSV, ABRIDGED)

# Persecution then and now

Felix, who was rather well informed about the Way... ordered the centurion to keep [Paul] in custody, but to let him have some liberty and not to prevent any of his friends from taking care of his needs. Some days later when Felix came with his wife Drusilla, who was Jewish, he sent for Paul and heard him speak concerning faith in Christ Jesus. And as he discussed justice, self-control, and the coming judgement, Felix became frightened and said, 'Go away for the present; when I have an opportunity, I will send for you.' At the same time he hoped that money would be given to him by Paul, and for that reason he used to send for him very often and converse with him. After two years had passed, Felix was succeeded by Porcius Festus; and since he wanted to grant the Jews a favour, Felix left Paul in prison.

These four chapters of Acts have shown Paul repeatedly embracing danger and, like a good movie hero, managing somehow to escape from disaster at the last moment, often by the skin of his teeth. Although we are leaving the story in the middle, we leave with this hint that, ultimately, Paul's journey does not have a happy ending.

Paul's life is so different from our own lives day by day. After all, few of us have to contemplate facing martyrdom on a daily basis. There are still too many places in the world, however, where people do have to face danger each day for the sake of their faith. Paul's story might also remind us of those in 'first-world' countries who are incarcerated, not because they are criminals but because of poverty, racism, sexism and all kinds of prejudice and fear.

Leaving Paul abandoned in this bleak prison, let us remember those who lose years of their lives to miscarriages of justice and take Paul's experience as an inspiration to pray and act and work for those who are abandoned in prisons or persecuted for their faith.

### Prayer

*Lord, help me to find out how I can act on behalf of those who are incarcerated or persecuted unjustly.*

MAGGI DAWN

# Praying with Psalm 19

When we pray, we address God as 'Our Father in heaven...', but how do we know him and how do we know what he is like, what kind of person he is?

Psalm 19 is a psalm of two halves, two sides of the coin. The first part (vv. 1–6) encourages us to look up to the heavens, because they 'declare the glory of God' (v. 1). One way we can know what God is like is to see what he has done in creation, 'the work of his hands' (v. 1). This is the God (Hebrew: *el*) of might and power, the one who in the beginning created heaven and the earth (Genesis 1:1). This is the God who prompts us (in the words of the hymn translated by Stuart Hine) to 'consider all the works Thy hand hath made' and respond, 'How great Thou art!'

The second part of the psalm (vv. 7–14) encourages us to consider a different revelation of God. Instead of looking up to the skies, we are to look into a book; instead of considering what he has done, we are to meditate on what he has said. Doing so, we discover that God is not only global, great and glorious but also personal, pure and precious. This is the God (Hebrew: *Yahweh*) whom we can know by having a personal relationship with him. His words can turn our lives round, bringing refreshment and renewal to us as whole beings ('refreshing the soul', v. 7).

Thus, this psalm takes us on a journey. The great and powerful God who created the glory of the skies speaks to the whole world through his creation and that same God speaks to us personally as we read his words. As he speaks, we can respond, so that we enter into a relationship with him: he becomes our 'Rock and our Redeemer' (v. 14).

Let me invite you to pray with Psalm 19 and take the same journey. This psalm suggests principles of prayer that can guide us in our daily encounters with God: we can think globally and personally; we can consider creation and then read God's word; we can look to him for security and forgiveness. His promise is that we will be refreshed. May that be true for you this coming week.

*Stephen Rand*

# Global glory

> The heavens declare the glory of God; the skies proclaim the work of his hands. Day after day they pour forth speech; night after night they reveal knowledge. They have no speech, they use no words; no sound is heard from them. Yet their voice goes out into all the earth, their words to the ends of the world.

Our house faces west, so, as we sit on our sofa in the evening, we can, weather permitting, glimpse some glorious sunsets. On that same sofa, while writing these notes, I have repeatedly seen the promise that the coming winter will bring the best displays of the Northern Lights for many years (usually attached to an advert for an expensive icy holiday opportunity). Then I recall a night in Paraguay many years ago, the nearest streetlights hundreds of miles away, so that the sky was ablaze with stars and the Milky Way looked as if it had been splashed across the heavens with a paintbrush.

You will have your own memories of when simply raising your eyes has provoked a deep sense of awe, a recognition of God's glory. It is wonderful that we can have an almost daily reminder of the creator, simply by opening our eyes. No sound, just sight.

Yet, the psalmist says, this silent witness is vastly eloquent. It can be heard across the globe, it is universal and it is available to all. The apostle Paul echoes the same thought: 'Ever since God created the world, his invisible qualities, both his eternal power and his divine nature, have been clearly seen; they are perceived in the things that God has made' (Romans 1:20, GNB).

What 'knowledge' of God is displayed by the heavens? Many have seen his power in the lightning flash, his creative extravagance in the multitudes of the stars, his dependency in the daily sunrise, his glory in the glowing sunset.

Begin your journey of prayer today. Look up—yes, even on a Monday in November—and see what God is saying to you.

## Prayer

*Lord, as people around the world open their eyes and see your creation, open their minds so that they may see you in all that you have made.*

STEPHEN RAND

# Here comes the sun

In the heavens God has pitched a tent for the sun. It is like a bridegroom coming out of his chamber, like a champion rejoicing to run his course. It rises at one end of the heavens and makes its circuit to the other; nothing is deprived of its warmth.

This psalm was written when many of the tribes and cultures surrounding the people of God worshipped the sun or a god represented by the sun. There was an obvious logic to this: the sun clearly provided the light and warmth essential to life, and it could not safely be viewed directly by the human eye. It is even possible that the psalm uses language and imagery taken from these sun-worshipping cultures. If that is true, it only serves to reinforce the writer's conviction of the greatness of God: the sun, awesome as it is, is still no more than another of the Creator God's masterpieces.

It is almost as if the psalmist had an insight into the vastness of the universe when he describes the heavens as being like a tent. It is a wonderfully domestic image. It is followed by two further images: the resplendent bridegroom emerging in his glorious finery and the champion athlete exhilarated by running and completing the course.

It is not that God is like the sun but that the sun reveals something further of the character of God: splendid, exuberant, dependable, constant and life-giving. The sun is there for everyone and everything: 'nothing is deprived of its warmth' (v. 6). Have you noticed how everything looks better when the sun is out? The grimmest urban landscape, the scrubbiest rural backwater—all are improved by the sun.

One December, my wife Susan and I drove to Italy. For a whole Sunday afternoon, we had the site of the cathedral and leaning tower of Pisa to ourselves. They glowed with the reflection of glorious winter sunshine, which slowly went from yellow to gold to the deepest red. It was an eloquent, memorable and, yes, spiritual experience.

### Prayer

*Almighty and glorious God, fill my life with your Spirit so that I can reflect your glory, your beauty and your warmth into a world of darkness.*

STEPHEN RAND

# Sweeter than honey

The law of the Lord is perfect, refreshing the soul. The statutes of the Lord are trustworthy, making wise the simple. The precepts of the Lord are right, giving joy to the heart. The commands of the Lord are radiant, giving light to the eyes. The fear of the Lord is pure, enduring forever. The decrees of the Lord are firm, and all of them are righteous. They are more precious than gold, than much pure gold; they are sweeter than honey, than honey from the honeycomb. By them your servant is warned; in keeping them there is great reward.

At first glance, these verses sound like a poet in love, finding so many ways to say the same thing! With this very good poet, however, each restatement of the basic truth adds a new layer of meaning, produces a new facet on the brilliantly cut diamond.

First, he describes the core qualities of God's word (to the writer this would have been the Torah, the first five books of the Bible). It is perfect, trustworthy, right, radiant, pure, firm—more precious than gold, sweeter than honey. Then he describes what God's word gives to the reader—refreshment, wisdom, joy, light and warning. Is that your experience? I hope that reading these notes each day is not so much a chore or a duty as a source of refreshment and joy. When you love someone, hearing from them is never a burden. As part of your daily prayer journey, ask God to make his word come alive to you by his Spirit.

I work for Open Doors, an organisation that began with Brother Andrew, 'God's Smuggler', taking incredible risks to deliver Bibles to believers facing persecution behind the Iron Curtain. Some 50 years later, there are still Christians suffering for their faith and many are still just as keen to have their own Bible, so the smuggling and the risk-taking continue. It is a reminder that God's word is more precious than gold. When you are facing suffering and danger for the one you love, you are even more desperate to hear from them.

### Prayer

*Lord, may your word be like honey on my lips. May the sweetness of your presence remain with me day by day.*

STEPHEN RAND

# Guilty until proved innocent

But who can discern their own errors? Forgive my hidden faults.
Keep your servant also from wilful sins; may they not rule over me.
Then I will be blameless, innocent of great transgression.

Here is human reality: if 'the unfolding of your words gives light' (Psalm 119:130), then it will show up things we may prefer were left in darkness—just as the sun has that nasty habit of revealing all the smears on the windows. Verse 6 of this psalm is literally translated as 'nothing is hidden from its heat'.

One version of a recurring story tells of a bishop who had six objectionable curates and did not know how to get rid of them. He sent each one an anonymous letter saying, 'All is discovered. Flee.' And they all fled!

We live in a society that is obsessed with attempting to present a controlled self-image… and also with gossip about those who fail and whose secrets emerge. Christians have always known that nothing can be hidden from God, though, sadly, they do not always live as though that were true.

These verses cover every type of wrongdoing—the things we do that we do not even understand; the secret sins; the things we do wilfully. Many times we may have echoed the psalmist's prayer for freedom: 'may they not rule over me' (v. 13). Luckily, the grace and mercy of God breaks the chains of sin, so Paul could write emphatically, 'Sin shall no longer be your master, for you are not under the law but under grace' (Romans 6:14).

We may long to be regarded as blameless and innocent and that can be our reality, because of what Jesus has done. God 'chose us in him before the creation of the world to be holy and blameless in his sight… In [Christ] we have redemption through his blood, the forgiveness of sins, in accordance with the riches of God's grace' (Ephesians 1:4–7). What good news!

### Reflection

*Our daily prayer should always include confession. Each day, as we recognise our failings, we can also praise God for the forgiveness we receive.*

STEPHEN RAND

# Pleasing God

> May these words of my mouth and this meditation of my heart be
> pleasing in your sight.

This is the prayer of the preacher as he or she stands up to speak—or
at least it should be! The time spent in preparation is not to ensure a
polished oration; it is to hear from God so there is something to pass
on from him. That is why it was my prayer before writing these notes.

It is a prayer of humility. The psalmist was a gifted poet, yet his concern was with ensuring that what he wrote would be pleasing to God,
not his readers or listeners. He did not rely on his gifting, but sought
God's help as he used his gifts. The psalm goes beyond a simple skill
with words. The word translated 'meditation', for example, is rare in
scripture: in one of the few other places it is used, it is instead translated as 'plotting'. This captures the idea of careful, focused thought
with an end in view. It is thought that comes from the heart, the innermost being.

Too many of my prayers come quickly from my brain rather than
thoughtfully from my heart. Sometimes I just verbalise what is worrying
me and ask God to sort it out. This verse reminds me that God is looking for more from being in relationship with me. He is the life-giving
Creator; he breathes his Spirit into his people; he speaks to us through
his Word. This should prompt us to give time to reflecting on his words
so that they become part of our lives, so our heart can touch God's
heart. Then we can be sure that our meditations will be pleasing in his
sight, 'for the mouth speaks what the heart is full of' (Luke 6:45).

This is not a meditation that seeks to empty our minds. Rather, it is
about immersing ourselves in the task and the joy of spending time in
God's presence so that our lives are shaped by him.

### Prayer

*Loving Father, let my prayers reflect what is in your heart rather than
simply inform you what is in mine. May your will be done; may your
kingdom come on earth.*

STEPHEN RAND

103

# My Rock and my Redeemer

May these words of my mouth and this meditation of my heart be pleasing in your sight, Lord, my Rock and my Redeemer.

The psalm comes to an end. The powerful Creator God whose glory blazes in the heavens knows me as an individual. The one who speaks to the whole world hears when I speak to him, and is willing to be my God as well as the God of the universe.

The psalmist uses two words to describe how he relates to God. The first is 'rock'. It is a word used many times in the psalms. In Psalm 40:2, for example, we have the words, 'He lifted me out of the slimy pit, out of the mud and the mire; he set my feet on a rock and gave me a firm place to stand.' David, to whom this psalm is credited, knew what it was like to spend years on the run, skulking in caves. His lack of self-control led him into adultery and murder and cost him a baby son. His adult son attacked him with an army. His best friend died young. He needed a rock, a place of spiritual safety and security. He found that rock in God and through God.

Whether we feel as if the whole world is disintegrating or it is just confusing, painful or disastrous, God is reaching out his hand to us, offering himself as the refuge from the storm: 'My health may fail, and my spirit may grow weak, but God remains the strength of my heart' (Psalm 73:26, NLT).

God is also our redeemer. What God did for the people of Israel he can do for you: he brought them out of slavery and set them free. The redeemer was the one who paid the price, who bought them back. In Jewish Law, he was a kinsman, a member of the family.

Jesus paid the price: he bought us back from the grip and punishment of sin and set us free, making us part of his family, the family of God.

### Prayer
*Dear Lord, thank you for the security and salvation I find in you. Help me to help others discover you can be their Rock and their Redeemer.*

STEPHEN RAND

# The Good Shepherd

Not so long ago, a kind nun explained to me what it meant to have a 'special devotion' (in faith terms). I had sometimes wondered about the significance of the titles common in the Roman Catholic Church—what it meant for nuns to describe themselves as 'Sister Margaret [or whoever] of the Holy Cross' or 'of the Sacred Heart'. My friend told me that such titles signified the 'special devotion' of the nun concerned—that is, an aspect of Christian belief or episode or character in the gospel story that most inspired their faith and prayers.

Intrigued by this, I began to wonder what *my* 'special devotion' might be. As a long-standing employee of the Bible Reading Fellowship, surely the Bible would be the most appropriate response in my case? What about God the Father or Mary the mother of Jesus, seeing as I have written a fair bit about parenting, the love of God and related ideas?

Then, as I prayed one day, it came to me: the Good Shepherd. Of course! As far back as I can remember, I have loved stories and pictures inspired by the biblical idea of God as shepherd, caring for us, his flock. When I was very small, my mother would sing me to sleep with a Victorian bedtime prayer: 'Jesus, tender Shepherd, hear me/Bless your little lamb tonight'. Psalm 23 was the first psalm I ever learned and is still one of my favourites. Still, reflecting on the patience, gentle care and security symbolised by the Good Shepherd remains a rich source of consolation and inspiration for me.

Over the next few days, we will reflect on some of the Good Shepherd passages from the Old and New Testaments. These include some famously lovely words, but they can become overly familiar if we forget their wider context and read them purely to apply to ourselves. We should not forget, either, that being a shepherd was, and often still is, a solitary, arduous and occasionally dangerous job. Both sheep and shepherd are vulnerable—and both need each other.

A final thought: as you read, you may find the Good Shepherd to be a particularly meaningful image for you, too. If not, you could try prayerfully identifying your own 'special devotion'.

*Naomi Starkey*

# He is with us

The Lord is my shepherd, I shall not want. He makes me lie down in green pastures; he leads me beside still waters; he restores my soul. He leads me in right paths for his name's sake. Even though I walk through the darkest valleys, I fear no evil; for you are with me; your rod and your staff—they comfort me. You prepare a table before me in the presence of my enemies; you anoint my head with oil; my cup overflows. Surely goodness and mercy shall follow me all the days of my life, and I shall dwell in the house of the Lord my whole life long.

We begin with the quintessential Good Shepherd passage—best beloved of all the psalms, offering as it does the deepest reassurance that the Lord (YHWH in the original Hebrew, the mysterious and unpronounceable name of God) is with us. His presence sustains us, no matter what has happened, no matter where we are. The psalm begins and ends with reflection on God's loving care, while the imagery shifts from shepherd and sheep to guest and host at a lavish dinner party.

It is worth noting that while the psalm is tagged as being 'of David', some commentators interpret 'the house of the Lord' as referring to the temple, which was built after David's time. The temple was significant not only as the place of sacrifice and public and private prayer but also as the very visible symbol, in the middle of the city, of God's presence with his people.

At the heart of this psalm is the sobering thought that, despite the Shepherd's care, dark and dangerous places are unavoidable. The bad news is that, however well-behaved and careful we are, we will end up journeying through them at some point, because that is life and sometimes life is very hard. The good news is that, even in the most fearful circumstances, we are assured that we have a heavenly armed guard alongside us.

## Reflection

*Today is Advent Sunday, the start of the Church's yearly cycle of festivals and commemorations. Take time to read through Psalm 23 aloud, phrase by phrase, and wait in silence to hear God's gentle whisper in your heart.*

NAOMI STARKEY

# He cherishes us

Get you up to a high mountain, O Zion, herald of good tidings; lift up your voice with strength, O Jerusalem, herald of good tidings, lift it up, do not fear; say to the cities of Judah, 'Here is your God!' See, the Lord God comes with might, and his arm rules for him; his reward is with him, and his recompense before him. He will feed his flock like a shepherd; he will gather the lambs in his arms, and carry them in his bosom, and gently lead the mother sheep.

These verses are from the turning-point in the book of Isaiah, where judgment and despair turn to comfort and hope. The whole of Isaiah 40 is a profoundly poetic meditation on the grandeur and majesty of God, but here we find a wonderful juxtaposition of images—the coming of the mighty king who is also the gentle shepherd. We will reflect more tomorrow on the traditional connection between those two images in the culture of that time; today let us meditate on the tenderness of the one who picks up his lambs and cuddles them.

Depending on our personal experiences of being loved and looked after, we may find it either easy or not to imagine being held in a safe and secure embrace. Whatever our experiences, we may find it harder still to imagine that such intimacy can characterise our relationship with God. Yes, as Isaiah 40 tells us, God is sovereign, eternal, 'the Creator of the ends of the earth' (v. 28); yet, at the same time, he cherishes us with a love more enduring than that of any mother (49:15).

If we know we have neglected our relationship with God, we may end up so racked with guilt that we cannot bear to open our Bibles (or *New Daylight*), let alone pray. We may endure times so storm-tossed that we feel too damaged even to think about whether or not our faith can help us. That is when we can hold on to the knowledge that the Good Shepherd promises to hold us, carry us, cuddle us.

### Reflection

*'Do not fear, for I am with you, do not be afraid, for I am your God'*
*(Isaiah 41:10).*

NAOMI STARKEY

# He cares for us

For thus says the Lord God: I myself will search for my sheep, and will seek them out. As shepherds seek out their flocks when they are among their scattered sheep, so I will seek out my sheep. I will rescue them from all the places to which they have been scattered on a day of clouds and thick darkness. I will bring them out from the peoples and gather them from the countries, and will bring them into their own land; and I will feed them on the mountains of Israel, by the watercourses, and in all the inhabited parts of the land. I will feed them with good pasture, and the mountain heights of Israel shall be their pasture; there they shall lie down in good grazing land, and they shall feed on rich pasture on the mountains of Israel. I myself will be the shepherd of my sheep, and I will make them lie down, says the Lord God.

I wrote on verses from Ezekiel 34 in May last year, but (editor's privilege) wanted to include the selection above among our Good Shepherd passages. The dramatic book of Ezekiel is not as well known as it ought to be and today's passage is a beautiful evocation of God's care.

In the ancient Near East, shepherding was used as an image for the task of governing people as far back as the third millennium BC. Here, the Lord God is being the Good Shepherd, in contrast to the bad shepherds (kings) who had woefully failed to look after Israel. As a result, the people had been violently dispersed, exiled, far from the land of milk and honey. They had been lost, but now the Good Shepherd will bring them home and nurse them back to health.

This passage shows us that God cares not just for individuals but also for whole nations. We may rightly emphasise the importance of cultivating our individual relationship with the Shepherd, but what about the relationship between the Shepherd and our family, our community, our church, our country?

### Reflection

*The Lord is my shepherd; the Lord is our shepherd;
the Lord is your shepherd.*

NAOMI STARKEY

# He searches for us

Now all the tax-collectors and sinners were coming near to listen to him. And the Pharisees and the scribes were grumbling and saying, 'This fellow welcomes sinners and eats with them.' So he told them this parable: 'Which one of you, having a hundred sheep and losing one of them, does not leave the ninety-nine in the wilderness and go after the one that is lost until he finds it? When he has found it, he lays it on his shoulders and rejoices. And when he comes home, he calls together his friends and neighbours, saying to them, 'Rejoice with me, for I have found my sheep that was lost.' Just so, I tell you, there will be more joy in heaven over one sinner who repents than over ninety-nine righteous persons who need no repentance.'

The opening words of today's reading are a useful reminder that Jesus' teaching was not delivered in the first-century equivalent of the Sunday morning 'sermon slot', but out on the road, in the middle of everyday life and the heat of the day, surrounded by jostling crowds and irritated opponents.

The parable of the lost sheep is the first in a series of three such stories that focus on how Jesus' way was to connect with the 'sinners' whom the religious hierarchy wanted to exclude. His way meant connecting not in order to condemn but to welcome them and enjoy their company.

If, like me, you first encountered this story as a children's picture book, you may, like me, have thought of it as primarily being about the misadventures of a bad sheep who wilfully went astray. We may, as a result, find it surprising to rediscover that the real point is not the waywardness of the sheep but the tenacity of the shepherd. He is even ready to risk the entire flock (left not in a safe fold but 'in the wilderness') for the sake of the missing one. After the sheep has been found, there is communal rejoicing: all this for the sake of one single sheep.

### Reflection

*Do we believe that we matter that much to the Shepherd? Do we believe that those we find easy to label 'sinners' matter that much to him, too?*

NAOMI STARKEY

# He dies for us

'I am the good shepherd. The good shepherd lays down his life for the sheep. The hired hand, who is not the shepherd and does not own the sheep, sees the wolf coming and leaves the sheep and runs away—and the wolf snatches them and scatters them. The hired hand runs away because a hired hand does not care for the sheep.'

We must not forget how shocking Jesus' words would have sounded to their original audience. He is applying to himself imagery used by the prophets to refer to the Lord God. Rather than telling a story about a hypothetical good shepherd, he is here explicitly identifying *himself* as that shepherd, the true Good Shepherd of Israel.

This teaching follows the story of the healing of the man born blind, who was then rejected by the Pharisees (John 9). Together they point to the fact that the religious leaders were conspicuously failing in their pastoral duty of care for the people. The identity of the 'hired hand' (v. 12) who 'runs away' (v. 12)—in contrast to the good shepherd—therefore, would have been all too obvious to Jesus' listeners.

The good shepherd, Jesus says, is even willing to risk his own life to save his sheep from wild animals. These days, and in heavily urbanised countries, the threat of approaching wolves can sound more like a fairytale scenario than the harsh reality it would have been in New Testament times. Thinking about it, the hired hand's response sounds quite reasonable. After all, how prepared would we be to die to save an animal, even a favourite pet?

In this, we see that the love of the Good Shepherd for us, his sheep, is breathtaking in scope, beyond reason, extended to every one of us, whether we feel safe in the fold or straying, lost or found. It has the quality of selflessness that is the hallmark of true love, where nothing matters more to the lover than the well-being of the beloved and where love is lavished, whether or not a response is forthcoming.

## Reflection

*The perfect sacrifice looks away from self towards the other, largely unaware that there is any sacrifice.*

George Guiver et al., *Priests in a People's Church* (SPCK, 2001)

NAOMI STARKEY

# He knows all of us

'I am the good shepherd. I know my own and my own know me, just as the Father knows me and I know the Father. And I lay down my life for the sheep. I have other sheep that do not belong to this fold. I must bring them also, and they will listen to my voice. So there will be one flock, one shepherd.'

I like the joke about heaven where Peter is showing round a newcomer and they pass a closed door, from behind which singing can be heard. 'Who's in there?' asks the newcomer. 'Oh,' says Peter, 'that's the [insert denomination of choice]. They think they're the only ones here.'

Following on directly from yesterday's reading, our passage repeats and extends Jesus' words about his identity as the Good Shepherd. It is also a further rebuke to the listening Pharisees, who were obsessed with maintaining the 'purity' of 'their' flock and excluding the 'other'—in this case, the Gentiles. As with the response of the hired hand, the attitude is why should a hardworking shepherd expend effort on somebody else's flock? This, though, is yet another reminder of the scandalous generosity of God's love: it is really and truly limitless. There are no favourites, no hierarchies, no first and second class. Everybody is welcome.

Jealousy is one of the earliest emotions we know, especially if we have siblings close in age to us. We love to be loved, but it can be hard to accept that others have a right to share that love. The good news is that not only is God's love inexhaustible but also, as we are touched by his love, so we begin to be changed and learn to love as he does.

His love can enlarge the smallness of our hearts and the narrowness of our understanding of his grace.

### Reflection

*The Lord Jesus was sent to tell us that we are loved and that God has called us into the same intimacy that he shares with the Father and the Spirit. Caught up in that love we, too, are sent to love as we have been loved.*

Jean Marie Dwyer OP, *The Sacred Place of Prayer* (BRF, 2013)

NAOMI STARKEY

# As we follow his example

I exhort the elders among you to tend the flock of God that is in your charge, exercising the oversight, not under compulsion but willingly, as God would have you do it—not for sordid gain but eagerly. Do not lord it over those in your charge, but be examples to the flock. And when the chief shepherd appears, you will win the crown of glory that never fades away.

As I mentioned in the Introduction, shepherd and sheep need one another. The flock needs the shepherd's care and it is hard for the shepherd to be a shepherd without a flock to care for. Acknowledgment of this mutual dependence should, so today's Bible passage tells us, be at the heart of the relationship between church leaders and members. Rather than pursuing high office, wide influence or just lots of adulation, the ambition of a godly leader must focus on being a faithful and obedient servant. Of course, ministry work must be carried out competently and managed efficiently, but the foundational aim must always be nurturing the well-being of the flock and not enhancing the status of the shepherd. Any 'crown of glory' comes from God alone, at the end of all things.

In the Anglican ordination service, the bishop tells those about to ordained that they should always be mindful of the example of the Good Shepherd as they pursue their calling. These are not just generally inspiring words, but an essential part of mission. If church leaders fulfil their duty of demonstrating the love and care of the Good Shepherd to their people, in their turn the people will be enabled to demonstrate that love and care to one another and the wider world. As that happens, the world can look at the church (the body of Christ, 1 Corinthians 12:27) and glimpse a little of what God is like. That is why it is important we pray as often as we can for those who lead our churches and also for those who lead the leaders.

### Reflection

*May it one day be said of you, not necessarily that you talked about God cleverly, but that you made God real to people.*

Michael Ramsey, *The Christian Priest Today* (SPCK, 2009)

# Bible stories rediscovered: Ruth

Ruth is my favourite book in the Bible. It is an exquisite love story with elements of tragedy and intrigue, ending with a fascinating genealogy that is picked up at the beginning of the New Testament. I enjoy the relationships based on duty, trust, friendship and deep love that develop as the book progresses. While the book is named after Ruth, some might argue that the real heroine is Naomi: her trust in the Lord God, despite dreadful personal tragedy, is extraordinary. There have been times when I have gained encouragement from her honesty before God. Meanwhile, Ruth herself speaks words that have echoed in my own life. As a young woman choosing to follow Jesus rather than embrace the faith of my parents, I understood something of what it was to tell Christian friends, 'Your people will be my people and your God my God' (1:16).

The book has several fascinating aspects and I am indebted to Robert L. Hubbard Jr's *The New International Commentary on the Old Testament: Book of Ruth* (Eerdmans, 1988) for highlighting them. For example, Naomi and Boaz never actually meet, although their understanding of each other is central to the plot. The Lord God is rarely addressed and only at the very end does the author say that God enabled Ruth to conceive. There are no direct encounters with God and nowhere does God speak. This is a story in which God appears to be distant, yet the characters experience his grace and provision. The heroes and heroines are everyday people rather than great rulers. It is a reminder that God is aware of every intimate detail of our lives, whether or not we consider ourselves his people and wherever we live. The book of Ruth portrays individuals who make reasonable decisions (for example, Orpah and the guardian-redeemer) alongside others (Ruth and Boaz) who make sacrificial choices, demonstrating the kindness, faithfulness and generosity characteristic of God himself.

Finally, the book of Ruth offers an account of God saving the lives of ordinary women and men and thereby giving his people a king. As you prepare to celebrate the birth of the King of kings, allow God to speak to you this Advent through Ruth, reminding you of his goodness to his people then and now.

*Lakshmi Jeffreys*

# Tragedies

In the days when the judges ruled, there was a famine in the land. So a man from Bethlehem in Judah, together with his wife and two sons, went to live for a while in the country of Moab. The man's name was Elimelek, his wife's name was Naomi, and the names of his two sons were Mahlon and Kilion. They were Ephrathites from Bethlehem, Judah. And they went to Moab and lived there. Now Elimelek, Naomi's husband, died, and she was left with her two sons. They married Moabite women, one named Orpah and the other Ruth. After they had lived there about ten years, both Mahlon and Kilion also died, and Naomi was left without her two sons and her husband.

Tragedy always engenders a feeling of senselessness. If the event has no discernible cause, we cannot understand why it should happen. If someone or something is responsible, we agonise over how and why anyone could do such a thing.

In the Bible, apparently senseless tragedy is often the backdrop to God's actions. The last chapters of Genesis, for example, recount how famine in Canaan led to Joseph being reconciled to his father and brothers, but, before this, all of them went through significant suffering. Similarly, in today's passage, famine leads Elimelek, Naomi and their sons to Moab. The shock of Elimelek's death is followed by the joy of two weddings, but then further tragedy. By the final verse of the passage, Naomi is a lonely widow in a foreign country with no heirs. On the surface, we can imagine little worse yet this is the perfect setting for divine intervention by a gracious God.

In addition to being the time to open calendars and mark the final countdown to Christmas, Advent traditionally is a time to reflect on life and prepare for Jesus coming again. This season in the church's year is a reminder that, however good or bad things are in the world, God really is in control and one day will come to put everything right for ever.

## Reflection

*Remember, the tragedy of the events leading to Jesus' crucifixion and burial in the tomb resulted in God's most gracious and miraculous action: raising Jesus from death.*

LAKSHMI JEFFREYS

# Unswerving commitment

But Ruth replied, 'Don't urge me to leave you or to turn back from you. Where you go I will go, and where you stay I will stay. Your people will be my people and your God my God. Where you die I will die, and there I will be buried. May the Lord deal with me, be it ever so severely, if even death separates you and me.' When Naomi realised that Ruth was determined to go with her, she stopped urging her.

As already mentioned, a striking feature of the book of Ruth is that God is never directly addressed, and there are reports of his actions and encounters with his people rather than descriptions of them happening there and then. Yet, there is no doubt that God is influencing events and committed to the people in this story.

The Christian concept of grace comes from the Hebrew *hesed*. This word suggests loyalty, reliability, compassion and kindness. It characterises Yahweh, the Lord God. *Hesed*, or grace, is also meant to characterise God's people. As Yahweh has shown grace to his people by providing food for them, Naomi seeks God's grace for her daughters-in-law, urging them to return to their parents and marry again. Naomi herself wishes to go home to God's people. When the girls refuse to leave her, Naomi states that God has been responsible for all her losses and to stay with her might involve further calamity. Perhaps her sense is that God's grace, in which she firmly believes, is no longer for her; maybe this feeling is behind her bitter outcry in verses 11–13.

Orpah eventually obeys her mother-in-law; Ruth disobeys. Yet, in her refusal to leave Naomi, Ruth expresses extraordinary *hesed*. It is worth reading the verses preceding this passage (vv. 6–15) to put the full effect of her remarkable statement in context. Not only is Ruth showing commitment to her mother-in-law but she is also choosing loyalty to the Lord God. She is willingly giving up everything to follow Naomi and Naomi's God.

### Prayer

*Loving God, you demonstrate unswerving commitment to us. Please help us to recognise this and thereby show your grace to others.*

LAKSHMI JEFFREYS

115

# Coming home

So the two women went on until they came to Bethlehem. When they arrived in Bethlehem, the whole town was stirred because of them, and the women exclaimed, 'Can this be Naomi?' 'Don't call me Naomi,' she told them. 'Call me Mara, because the Almighty has made my life very bitter. I went away full, but the Lord has brought me back empty. Why call me Naomi? The Lord has afflicted me; the Almighty has brought misfortune upon me.'

The following true story is retold with permission. Tom experienced a series of significant bereavements and had seemingly lost everyone and everything he held dear. He decided the God he had grown up with from childhood was not one he wanted to follow as an adult. Homeless and feeling suicidal, Tom was found by a Christian who paid for him to stay in a Christian centre. The people there showed Tom kindness and respect, despite Tom's refusal to engage with them or participate in any activities, particularly prayer and worship.

One day, an elderly woman arrived. She was not a Christian but was accompanied by Christians who were involved in the centre's activities. The woman's frail health meant that she needed someone to stay with her. Tom reluctantly agreed to be that person and was soon plied with questions, especially about his lost Christian faith. He answered honestly and, to his amazement he found himself telling the woman about God's love for her, even though he himself did not believe in this God! When the woman's friends returned, they discovered a new Christian and a bemused Tom. Some time later, Tom's own faith was rekindled.

Unlike Tom, Naomi did not lose her faith in God, but she lost her faith in God being good to her personally. Nevertheless, Naomi's honesty about God and her willingness to live among God's people brought Ruth to faith in this God and to live among God's people herself. Tom's honesty about God, despite his bitterness and anger about all that had happened to him, brought the elderly woman to faith.

### Reflection

*If we are honest to and about God, particularly in tough times, how might God use our stories?*

LAKSHMI JEFFREYS

# Introducing Boaz

Now Naomi had a relative on her husband's side, a man of standing from the clan of Elimelek, whose name was Boaz. And Ruth the Moabite said to Naomi, 'Let me go to the fields and pick up the leftover grain.' Naomi said to her, 'Go ahead my daughter.' So she went out, entered a field and began to glean behind the harvesters. As it turned out, she was working in a field belonging to Boaz, who was from the clan of Elimelek.

In yesterday's reading Naomi could not see beyond the tragedy of her situation. Ruth is not a victim of circumstances, though, and asks for permission to provide food for herself and Naomi. This is a brave move as she is an outsider, described as 'the Moabite'. It is perhaps the equivalent of Ruth being a black woman in a predominantly white town in one of the southern states in the USA. Ruth appears to be aware of her vulnerable position: she is a foreigner; a widow; a woman with even less status than her mother-in-law. Given her circumstances, she shows extraordinary faith as she accepts that there might be someone in whose eyes she might find favour.

As readers of the story, we are given a glimpse of God's broader perspective and introduced to someone new. Boaz comes from the same clan or tribe as Naomi's dead husband, is a man of influence and owns land, so stands in stark contrast to the women, who have arrived with no material possessions and no social standing. As yet, the significance of Boaz in the proceedings is unclear. Nonetheless, there is a suggestion that God has not abandoned Naomi as she has feared. Naomi and Ruth have chosen to get on with life among God's people, so they have increased their chances of experiencing personally the grace and provision of their God.

Sometimes we feel overwhelmed by difficulties. On other occasions, we have to get on with everyday life. In either case, we might choose to exercise humble trust in God and discover that God really is with us.

### Prayer

*Thank you, God, that you do not forsake us, but watch over our coming and going now and for evermore (see Psalm 121).*

LAKSHMI JEFFREYS

# Good character

Just then Boaz arrived from Bethlehem and greeted the harvesters, 'The Lord be with you!' 'The Lord bless you!' they answered. Boaz asked the overseer of his harvesters, 'Who does that young woman belong to?' The overseer replied, 'She is the Moabite who came back from Moab with Naomi. She said, "Please let me glean and gather among the sheaves behind the harvesters." She came into the field and has remained here from morning till now, except for a short rest in the shelter.'

The hero of the story finally makes an entrance and greets his harvest workers in the name of the living God. It is significant that, although God's hand over proceedings is only inferred at each stage, all the main players are allied with God.

In this passage, our hero Boaz catches a glimpse of our heroine. It is not clear what about Ruth has attracted Boaz's attention, but he does not recognise her as one of the workers he has hired. He therefore asks his foreman about her, to see who she works for.

The foreman's response is full. Here is the young woman from Moab. Everyone has heard about her faithfulness to her mother-in-law. Now she has displayed courage and integrity by asking permission not just to glean at the edges of the field, as the law allows, but to gather behind Boaz's other workers. This audacity is yet another indication of Ruth's good character: she wants more than the bare minimum for herself and Naomi and is honest about it. Perhaps she has been waiting in the field because only Boaz himself can grant her request. In the meantime, her good character has become apparent to a number of people.

President Abraham Lincoln said, 'Character is like a tree and reputation like a shadow.' In other words, what we are known for is determined by who we are, what we are like when no one is watching. For Christians, the fruit of the Spirit is love, joy, peace, forbearance, kindness, goodness, faithfulness, gentleness and self-control (Galatians 5:22–23), visible signs of our character.

**Prayer**

*O Lord, may people see the fruit of your Spirit in my life today.*

LAKSHMI JEFFREYS

# Boaz and Ruth

Boaz said to Ruth, 'My daughter, listen to me. Don't go and glean in another field and don't go away from here. Stay here with the women who work for me. Watch the field where the men are harvesting, and follow along after the women. I have told the men not to lay a hand on you. And whenever you are thirsty, go and get a drink from the water jars the men have filled.' At this, she bowed down with her face to the ground. She asked him, 'Why have I found such favour in your eyes that you notice me—a foreigner?'

As an incurable romantic, every time I read this story I itch for Boaz and Ruth to meet. When the moment comes, Boaz is generous and clear, offering Ruth protection and sustenance. Ruth is almost overcome by the magnitude of his kindness. She wanted to find favour in someone's eyes and has found favour indeed in his: the respected landowner takes under his wing the vulnerable foreigner. All of us who love the genre have seen that kind of film!

So many close relationships today involve people looking out for themselves. Acts of kindness and generosity are not unknown, but the human tendency is to put our own needs first. So often our actions are influenced by what other people will think or what we might gain as a result of doing or saying something. We have no indication as to Boaz's motives, but in providing so much for Ruth, he risks alienating those around him who are opposed to outsiders.

We, too, might worry that there will not be enough for local people, never mind foreigners. What might happen if too many people come because we develop a reputation as a 'soft touch'? Once we trust not 'who' we are but 'whose' we are, recalling God's infinite love for us, we, like Boaz, can risk putting others first.

## Reflection

*'In your relationships with one another, have the same mindset as Christ Jesus: who, being in very nature God, did not consider equality with God something to be used to his own advantage; rather, he made himself nothing by taking the very nature of a servant, being made in human likeness' (Philippians 2:5–7).*

LAKSHMI JEFFREYS

# Under his wings

Boaz replied, 'I've been told all about what you have done for your mother-in-law since the death of your husband—how you left your father and mother and your homeland and came to live with a people you did not know before. May the Lord repay you for what you have done. May you be richly rewarded by the Lord, the God of Israel, under whose wings you have come to take refuge.'

It appears that Boaz's generosity to Ruth is a direct result of Ruth's kindness to Naomi: you scratched Naomi's back, so I will scratch yours. In addition, Boaz would have been taking seriously his responsibility as one of the people of God to provide for the poor and foreigners by not gleaning to the edge of his fields (Leviticus 19:9–10). Ruth's obedience to the Lord God is even more significant, however. It is because she has chosen to serve an initially alien God, encountered through marriage and then bereavement, that Boaz is able to pray that God would reward her faithfulness.

Like Naomi earlier in the story, Boaz is aware of God's hand in all events. He offers a sense that God blesses the righteous and punishes the wicked (Psalm 145:4–5), but protection will be there for all who seek it. The image of God carrying his people as a mother eagle protects her fledgling (Exodus 19:4) is echoed as Jesus speaks of wanting to protect the people as a mother hen protects her brood (Matthew 23:37).

In fact, God freely offers care and protection to all who avail themselves of it. Throughout history, the Christian Church has, similarly, offered sanctuary to those fleeing tyranny or seeking justice, regardless of their religious beliefs or social background. In the last century, there are countless stories of Christians helping Jews escaping Nazi persecution. Today, local churches might offer support to refugees and asylum seekers who have escaped from oppressive regimes. It is worth remembering the times God has offered us protection and to ask God where we might reflect this care for others.

**Prayer**

*We pray for all who need God's protection—may they find security under the shadow of his wings.*

LAKSHMI JEFFREYS

RUTH 2:18–21 (NIV)

# Abundant provision

[Ruth's] mother-in-law saw how much she had gathered. Ruth also brought out and gave her what she had left over after she had eaten enough. Her mother-in-law asked her, 'Where did you glean today? Where did you work? Blessed be the man who took notice of you!' Then Ruth told her mother-in-law about the one at whose place she had been working. 'The name of the man I worked with today is Boaz,' she said. 'The Lord bless him!' Naomi said to her daughter-in-law. 'He has not stopped showing his kindness to the living and the dead.' She added, 'That man is our close relative; he is one of our guardian-redeemers.' Then Ruth the Moabite said, 'He even said to me, "Stay with my workers until they finish harvesting all my grain."'

Naomi is amazed by both the enormity of the harvest Ruth brings (perhaps the equivalent of a small sack of cement!) and the leftover cooked grain. In response, Naomi prays God's blessing on Boaz before and especially after she realises his identity. Boaz has demonstrated *hesed*, the remarkable loving kindness and grace offered by God and, it is hoped, God's people. Naomi also acknowledges Ruth's status, referring to Boaz as 'our' relative.

Recently I saw a news item about child poverty. There were stories of youngsters whose carers were unable to provide them with a nutritious cooked meal more than once every few weeks. Two children were interviewed about the positive differences made to their lives, especially their schoolwork, by a scheme offering their families free hot food.

At the time of writing, many people face job uncertainty and economic strains. Our church is one among many providing bags of food donated for those who might otherwise struggle to eat. While God's provision is always more than abundant, there remain people without sufficient means to feed themselves adequately. In times of adversity, Christians need, more than ever, to offer *hesed* to those around. It is then interesting to consider who our 'relatives' are.

### Prayer

*Lord God, we pray for those around us who do not have enough to eat and ask that we be generous, just as you are generous in providing for us.*

LAKSHMI JEFFREYS

# Enacting God's plan

One day Ruth's mother-in-law Naomi said to her, 'My daughter, I must find a home for you, where you will be well provided for. Now Boaz, with whose women you have worked, is a relative of ours. Tonight he will be winnowing barley on the threshing-floor. Wash, put on perfume, and get dressed in your best clothes. Then go down to the threshing-floor, but don't let him know you are there until he has finished eating and drinking. When he lies down, note the place where he is lying. Then go and uncover his feet and lie down. He will tell you what to do.'

Naomi now wants to bring about what she asked of God in 1:8–9: namely that Ruth will have a home where she will be 'well provided for' (3:1). It is interesting that there is no mention of God at this point. In fact, the two women could appear manipulative, as Ruth is to make herself look and smell enticing (in the dark her scent will be vital). She is also to wait until Boaz is in a good mood after a hearty meal and then note where he is to sleep. (It would be a disaster to end up with the wrong man!) Then Ruth is to lie at his uncovered feet, which will eventually get cold, causing Boaz to wake. The hoped-for outcome is that Boaz will make Ruth his wife, but, for Ruth, this plan is fraught with danger.

God does not expect us to be passive, but, instead, provides us with opportunities and choices. If we are aware of who God is and how God works as we make decisions and act, so we are likely to carry out God's plans. Identifying and pursuing God's way is often risky, however, especially when God is not obviously present. It is often helpful to write down our hopes and prayers. As we hold our circumstances before God and look back at how he has heard us in the past, we might discover that he is inviting us to answer our own prayers.

### Prayer

*Holy Spirit, we pray for courage to take the next step*
*to bring about change.*

LAKSHMI JEFFREYS

# The benefit of risk

When Boaz... was in good spirits, he went over to lie down at the far end of the grain pile. Ruth approached quietly, uncovered his feet and lay down. In the middle of the night something startled the man; he turned—and there was a woman lying at his feet!... 'I am your servant Ruth,' she said. 'Spread the corner of your garment over me...' 'The Lord bless you, my daughter,' he replied. 'This kindness is greater than that which you showed earlier... And now, my daughter, don't be afraid... All the people of my town know that you are a woman of noble character.'

Ruth plays her part to perfection and everything follows exactly as Naomi predicted. Ruth, however, also uses her own initiative. In asking Boaz to cover her with the corner of his garment, Ruth is not just asking for protection: rather than waiting for Boaz, she is proposing marriage! She echoes Boaz's prayer that God will shelter Ruth under his wings (2:12) and puts her faith to the test. Ruth's willingness to trust Naomi and put herself and her reputation in danger shows that her actions are not simply for personal gain. Boaz is clearly delighted, recognising that Ruth has chosen a marriage to benefit her family, rather than choosing a younger man for herself. He comments on her kindness and assures Ruth that her reputation as a woman of noble character remains intact.

It is a common saying that 'faith is spelt R-I-S-K'. It is by taking risks to further God's kingdom that we demonstrate our trust in God. We need to be clear that we are responding to the prompting of the Holy Spirit and our actions are not simply taken to make ourselves look good. In the 19th century, for example, Anthony Ashley-Cooper, who became Lord Shaftesbury, worked to outlaw life-threatening child labour. There was significant opposition to his proposals at the time, as they meant business owners would lose money. Ashley was a Christian, however, and knew that he might need to sacrifice his reputation in order to do God's will. Thanks to the risks he took, millions felt the benefit.

### Prayer

*Loving God, help me to demonstrate my faith in you by taking risks today as the Holy Spirit directs.*

LAKSHMI JEFFREYS

RUTH 3:12–15 (NIV)

# Dealing with the unexpected

[Boaz said] 'Although it is true that I am a guardian-redeemer of our family, there is another who is more closely related than I. Stay here for the night, and in the morning if he wants to do his duty as your guardian-redeemer, good; let him redeem you. But if he is not willing, as surely as the Lord lives I will do it. Lie here until morning.' So she lay at his feet until morning, but got up before anyone could be recognised; and he said, 'No one must know that a woman came to the threshing-floor.'

Just at the point in the story when we are about to prepare for a wedding announcement, there is a twist in the tale. Boaz is not the nearest relative: someone else might be legally entitled to acquire Elimelek's land and possessions, which include Ruth. Boaz continues to behave with integrity. He will do what he can, but if the other man decides to take what is lawfully his, Boaz will not allow personal feelings to prevent justice. He also continues to look after Ruth, ensuring that no one can accuse her of immoral behaviour and giving her an enormous quantity of grain as a parting gift. Naomi advises patience: there might be a hitch in their plan, but they can trust God to work through Boaz for the best outcome (see 3:18).

Things do not always work out as we expect, but when we trust God and act with integrity, the result will be better than we could imagine. Many years ago, I had to choose between pursuing a teaching career and continuing a voluntary project. There were no jobs in the area so, if I remained, I would have to find work to pay the bills, but I would lose the chance to gain experience in my profession. Having prayed with friends, our sense was that I should stay and wait for God's provision. Within a month of making the decision to stay, the local authority changed its ruling, allowing jobs to be created in my area. I could enjoy both a career and the voluntary work.

### Reflection

*'And we know that in all things God works for the good of those who love him, who have been called according to his purpose'* (Romans 8:28).

LAKSHMI JEFFREYS

# Choices

[Boaz said] 'Naomi, who has come back from Moab, is selling the piece of land that belonged to our relative Elimelek... I... suggest that you buy it in the presence of these seated here... For no one has the right to do it except you, and I am next in line.'... Then Boaz said, 'On the day you buy the land from Naomi, you also acquire Ruth the Moabite, the dead man's widow, in order to maintain the name of the dead with his property.' At this, the guardian-redeemer said, 'Then I cannot redeem it because I might endanger my own estate.'

Boaz clearly spells out the situation. Naomi is selling her husband's land. As a relative, but not as close as the other man, Boaz is offering the closer relative the chance to fulfil familial duties and buy the land. Boaz states at the outset that one or other of them needs to do this so as not to leave Naomi destitute. Given the opportunity to gain more land, the potential guardian-redeemer jumps at it. When Boaz explains that Ruth is also part of the deal, however, the man has to rethink. On the one hand, Ruth is quite a catch: everyone has heard about her courage and faithfulness so who would not want to marry her? On the other hand, the man already has a family. Were he to buy the land and marry Ruth, her children would inherit this land. In addition, he would have to provide for Naomi, Ruth and any further children. This would reduce the inheritance of his existing heirs and he cannot afford to lose what he already has.

In contrast, Boaz does not worry about the enormous expense of taking on a family as well as more land. He joyfully redeems the property and, more importantly, takes Ruth to be his wife. He gives what he has so that Naomi and Ruth should be cared for, once again demonstrating extraordinary grace. The community rejoices with him.

### Reflection

*Jesus said, 'whoever wants to save their life will lose it, but whoever loses their life for me and for the gospel will save it' (Mark 8:35). What would you do as a guardian-redeemer?*

LAKSHMI JEFFREYS

# A happy ending

So Boaz took Ruth and she became his wife. When he made love to her, the Lord enabled her to conceive, and she gave birth to a son. The women said to Naomi: 'Praise be to the Lord, who this day has not left you without a guardian-redeemer. May he become famous throughout Israel! He will renew your life and sustain you in your old age. For your daughter-in-law, who loves you and who is better to you than seven sons, has given him birth.' Then Naomi took the child in her arms and cared for him. The women living there said, 'Naomi has a son!'

The story that began with tragedy ends with joy. Naomi lost a husband and two sons in a foreign country, but now has a son in her homeland. Her bitterness has been transformed and she is content in ways she never imagined. Ruth's devotion to Naomi is exemplified as she allows Naomi to bring up her grandson as her own child. The Lord God, apparently absent throughout most of the book, is now clearly present. It is God who enables Ruth to conceive and the local women recognise and praise God for all his goodness to Naomi. Ruth and Naomi, who chose to follow God, even when he seemed to have abandoned them, have been rewarded for their faithfulness. They arrived in Bethlehem with nothing and now have status and an heir.

In a few days' time, we shall remember another woman who arrives in Bethlehem with very little, but through whom God gives his greatest gift to the world. Like Ruth, Mary shows courage, obedience and faithfulness and God blesses her beyond anything she might have imagined.

At various points in Luke's Gospel, Mary treasures events and ponders them in her heart. I can imagine Ruth and Naomi talking together about the years of sorrow and reflecting on God's provision for them. As you look back over the story of Ruth, perhaps you can reflect on your own life and God's provision for you. What memories do you treasure and ponder in your heart?

**Prayer**

*Take a break from your seasonal preparations and bring before God the events of the past year.*

LAKSHMI JEFFREYS

# Into the future

And they named him Obed. He was the father of Jesse, the father of David. This, then, is the family line of Perez: Perez was the father of Hezron, Hezron the father of Ram, Ram the father of Amminadab, Amminadab the father of Nahshon, Nahshon the father of Salmon, Salmon the father of Boaz, Boaz the father of Obed, Obed the father of Jesse, and Jesse the father of David.

The Bible contains a number of genealogies. The number of names and place of particular individuals has special significance in each case. Here Boaz is the seventh person—seven being an important number in Hebrew thinking. These lists of names are not to be read as a detailed family tree as the list spans several hundred years. Instead, it is worth recognising that there are characters whose stories are told at length in the Bible (Perez, Boaz, Jesse and, of course, King David) and others about whom virtually nothing is known. Regardless of their fame, each life has been key to God's purpose. A nice touch in this list is that it begins with Perez, who was named by the crowd of well-wishers when Boaz acquired Ruth as his wife (4:12). For the original hearers of the book of Ruth, however, the genealogy shows the result of God's faithfulness to a foreign woman who chose to follow the God of her mother-in-law and an upright man among God's people. An otherwise insignificant couple became the great-grandparents of Israel's greatest king.

Over the next few days, many of us are likely to hear or read a longer version of this genealogy at the beginning of Matthew's Gospel (Matthew 1:1–17). Ruth or Naomi could not possibly have imagined that their tenacity to God and God's people would be directly linked to the arrival of Jesus the Messiah. Our lives might resemble Naomi's or Ruth's at the beginning of this book: we might be rejoicing at God's goodness to us, Advent and Christmas might bring painful memories, or we might be overwhelmed with busyness with no time to think. However we are feeling as Christmas approaches, though, we can take encouragement that God is with us, even if he seems absent for now.

## Reflection
*Emmanuel, which means 'God with us'.*

LAKSHMI JEFFREYS

# Holy family, human family

In the years after Jesus ascended into heaven, four men were inspired by God to write an account of his life and teachings. Their work became the four Gospels.

Mark and John decided to start their accounts of the life of Jesus with his baptism by John in the Jordan. John, in addition, gave us his famous prologue to provide an amazing cosmic scene-setting for the story. Matthew and Luke, however, gathered stories of his birth and decided to record these for us. It is because of these two evangelists that we have the very well-known tales of stables, angels, shepherds and kings. As people go round the shopping malls this year and hear the carols and see crib scenes on cards, giftwrapping and window displays, it is Matthew and Luke they must thank.

There is an undeniable magic about Christmas and, for all the usual Christian tut-tutting at the commercialisation of it, most of us love the fact that, at this rather bleak time of year (for those of us in the northern hemisphere), we have a story that people of every race, tribe and nation are drawn to and warmed by. It is a story that gives rise to the most elaborate festivities, meals, gifts and holidays. These are such that you would think the story they are supposed to be celebrating must be one full of celebrities and megastars, but, in fact, it centres on a very human family. That family, however, had an encounter with an extraordinary God who did something so significant through it that the world was changed forever.

In these coming days of Christmas, we shall once again visit the young mum and her caring husband and their bright young child. In the midst of the busy round of celebrations, we have an opportunity to take moments of quiet and return in our hearts to that family scene, so that we can discover them again as a holy family with a holy message for our world so darkened by all that is far from holy.

*Michael Mitton*

# The family tree

This is the genealogy of Jesus the Messiah the son of David, the son of Abraham... and Jacob [was] the father of Joseph, the husband of Mary, and Mary was the mother of Jesus who is called the Messiah. Thus there were fourteen generations in all from Abraham to David, fourteen from David to the exile to Babylon, and fourteen from the exile to the Messiah.

This genealogy is not the most exciting of starts to a Gospel. Readers of Matthew have to wade through a dense pile of Old Testament names and, by the time you get to Shealtiel and Zerubbabel, you may have all but given up. This is how we, in the 21st century, might view it, but for many in the first century, it would have made their eyes light up with delight! Perhaps the nearest we get to understanding this is the current interest in ancestry, as illustrated by the popularity of the TV programme *Who Do You Think You Are?* In each episode, a celebrity starts to sift through his or her family history and discovers all kinds of stories. Something about these stories often moves them to tears, because through them they feel a close bond with their forebears. They know they still carry something of that family history in their veins and something of that history will continue into the future.

It is this kind of history that Matthew is detailing in this genealogy. Joseph may seem like an ordinary carpenter, but we are invited to take a look at where he has come from and discover that he has royal blood in his veins. In the minds of those early readers, it provides good credentials for Joseph and Jesus. For us today, there is the message that, no matter who may be in our particular family story, we all have links to that child born in Bethlehem. In a truly wondrous way, he has made us children of God, and so, in a figurative sense, there is royal blood in our veins too.

### Prayer

*Father, you have set me in a human family for my life here on earth, but you have also placed me in a holy family, founded by Christ, and made me an heir in your royal household.*

MICHAEL MITTON

# In the family way

But the angel said to her, 'Do not be afraid, Mary; you have found favour with God. You will conceive and give birth to a son, and you are to call him Jesus. He will be great and will be called the Son of the Most High. The Lord God will give him the throne of his father David, and he will reign over the house of Jacob forever; his kingdom will never end.' 'How will this be,' Mary asked the angel, 'since I am a virgin?'

After telling us about Zechariah and Elizabeth at the start of his Gospel, Luke introduces us to Joseph and Mary, who are betrothed (v. 27)—that is, in a legally binding relationship in which intercourse was not permitted until the marriage ceremony. Luke tells us very little about these two: he does not extol them as virtuous or exceptional in any particular way.

Then Mary is visited by Gabriel and this great angel declares her 'highly favoured', an accolade with which Mary clearly struggles (vv. 28–29). In an apparently calm manner, Gabriel explains that this young girl will miraculously conceive a son and he will be none other than the child of God and will live for ever. It is impossible to imagine what must have gone on in Mary's mind at this point. One moment she was probably doing something like the laundry and the next she was being told that she was to carry the child of God! Not only is this a fairly major piece of news, but there is the matter of having to explain the pregnancy to Joseph and the family.

It is therefore all the more impressive that Mary only asks one practical question (v. 34) and, in response to the answer, simply says, 'I am the Lord's servant' (v. 38). In those few words, this young teenager shows what she is truly made of. No matter how impossible or terrifying these words of God, Mary's one desire is simply to be available to God for his purposes on earth. Her practical question and her faithful agreement show that she was a wonderful mix of human and holy.

### Reflection

*How much are you willing to let God ask of you?*

MICHAEL MITTON

MATTHEW 1:20–21 (TNIV)

# The head of the family

But after [Joseph] had considered this, an angel of the Lord appeared to him in a dream and said, 'Joseph son of David, do not be afraid to take Mary home as your wife, because what is conceived in her is from the Holy Spirit. She will give birth to a son, and you are to give him the name Jesus, because he will save his people from their sins.'

We can only imagine the distress that Joseph would have been in when he discovered that his betrothed was pregnant. No doubt she attempted to explain the angel's visitation and the reason for her pregnancy, but it seems that initially it was just too far-fetched for Joseph, who must surely have assumed she had been with another man. He could have responded angrily, but instead he plans to divorce her privately (v. 19), which gives us an insight into the depth of his love and respect for Mary: he does not want to harm her good name.

There is no sense of divine disapproval at Joseph's failure to believe Mary's story. In fact, heaven gives him a helping hand by sending an angel to him, and the first thing the angel does is remind him of his ancestry: 'Joseph, son of David' (v. 20). Heaven views him as a descendant of David, that great man of faith; it does not view him as a doubter. He is then told not to be afraid to take Mary as his wife, for he feared both divine and public disapproval. He is told that the cause of her pregnancy is the Holy Spirit and, from then on, Joseph is a confident believer. Finally, the angel gives Joseph the task assigned to the head of the family—to name the child, giving him a name that is to do with salvation.

Right at the start, this little family discover God to be a God of grace, who calls Mary 'highly favoured' and Joseph 'son of David'. There is no reference to their human failings, and the name of their child is to do with salvation and rescue, not punishment and judgment. Holiness is rooted in grace.

### Prayer

*Thank you, Lord, that, as you visit the human race, you treat us with*
*dignity and call us into the pathways of grace.*

MICHAEL MITTON

# Family ties

In those days Caesar Augustus issued a decree that a census should be taken of the entire Roman world... And everyone went to their own town to register. So Joseph also went up from the town of Nazareth in Galilee to Judea, to Bethlehem the town of David, because he belonged to the house and line of David. He went there to register with Mary, who was pledged to be married to him and was expecting a child.

We might wonder what went through their minds. Thus far it cannot have been an easy ride for Mary and Joseph. They believed that Mary carried the child of God, but it is unlikely that many others shared their belief, so it must have been a lonely time for this family. Then comes the news that they have to travel the long journey to Judea in Mary's final weeks of pregnancy, because of Joseph's family ties with David. Although the journey was only 80 miles, in those days it would have been painful and arduous—definitely not what a young mum-to-be would want to be doing.

We only know the barest details of this story and are given no clue as to what was going on in the minds of the couple as they journeyed south. No doubt they clung to the reassurance given by the angels; Mary had declared that she was the Lord's servant (Luke 1:38), so, presumably, was prepared to serve him even when it hurt. It is also quite likely that they knew the child of God had to be born in Bethlehem: it was the assigned birthplace of the Messiah (Micah 5:2; Matthew 2:3–8), so this new member of the family must be born in the city of David. It is admirable that Mary and Joseph show such faith and courage. It is also wonderful that God should place such trust in these two vulnerable humans. In this way, among other things, Christmas is a celebration of God choosing to work with our broken and fallible humanity to bring about his holy purposes for our imperfect world.

### Prayer
*Our Saviour Christ is born. Let heaven and earth rejoice!*

MICHAEL MITTON

# A new member of the family

*While they were there, the time came for the baby to be born, and she gave birth to her firstborn, a son. She wrapped him in cloths and placed him in a manger, because there was no guest room available for them.*

As if the journey was not arduous enough, there was another problem to greet the family in Bethlehem: it was very busy. We may know that sinking feeling when we go shopping before Christmas and the crowds seem overwhelming: there is nowhere to park and there are queues for everything. Well, it was, of course, many times worse for a young mum-to-be, about to give birth. Finally they find an inn with some room in its stable, which was probably the ground floor of a two-storey building where people lived upstairs and animals below.

It is far from ideal and not particularly hygienic, but Mary and Joseph decide it is the best they can hope for and they wait in this dark place, with the sounds of the busy city around them. How long they wait, we do not know, but finally the time comes when the young Mary feels the pains that are the beginning of labour. We do not know whether it was a short or long labour, but the baby boy arrives and it may have surprised Mary and Joseph to see that he looked like any other newborn. As far as we know, there was nothing to mark him out as a child fathered by God Almighty. Anyone coming into that stable to park their donkey would have seen a sight that was common in any family home—proud, tired parents with their tiny baby.

We are probably accustomed to preachers making points about this humble start for the Son of God, but we should seek to take our own moments to appreciate again the sheer wonder of God's decision to make such an unlikely entry into our world. In that wonder, we can let our hearts explore the implications of this and our spirits rise to worship the newborn king.

### Reflection

*What, for you, is the significance of God coming to earth in this way?*

MICHAEL MITTON

# The family welcomes shepherds

So [the shepherds] hurried off and found Mary and Joseph, and the baby, who was lying in the manger. When they had seen him, they spread the word concerning what had been told them about this child, and all who heard it were amazed at what the shepherds said to them. But Mary treasured up all these things and pondered them in her heart. The shepherds returned, glorifying and praising God for all the things they had heard and seen, which were just as they had been told.

A nativity play would not be the same without a host of small shepherds wearing dressing-gowns and towels fixed in place on their heads with cord. It is hard to tell quite what these children make of it when very few of them will meet shepherds nowadays, let alone ones from Israel.

Some imaginative playwrights may therefore look for modern equivalents, and probably the nearest would be refuse collectors. They are industrious people who serve us well, but we might not want to rush to give them a hug as we might worry about getting dirty. Similarly, because shepherds then worked in the mucky fields, handling animals all day, and could not attend the various purification ceremonies, they were regarded as being literally and spiritually unclean. So, to have them, of all people, turn up in your nursery would be somewhat alarming. Instinctively Mary and Joseph would want to protect their little child.

Tantalisingly, we do not know how they responded when the door creaked open and the smell of sheep filled the room, but the impression given is that those shepherds were made to feel very welcome in the stable. Then, after they left, there was much treasuring and pondering going on in Mary's heart.

The shepherds were in no doubt that they had witnessed a holy family, but you get the sense, too, that, as Mary pondered this visit, she was getting a glimpse of how these shepherds looked through God's eyes. Despite their appearance and despite what the legalists might say, there were clear signs that holiness was springing to life in those shepherd hearts of faith.

### Prayer

*Lord, let me see with your eyes, that I may treasure and I may ponder.*

MICHAEL MITTON

# A family trip to the temple

*When the time came for the purification rites required by the Law of Moses, Joseph and Mary took him to Jerusalem to present him to the Lord (as it is written in the Law of the Lord, 'Every firstborn male is to be consecrated to the Lord'), and to offer a sacrifice in keeping with what is said in the Law of the Lord: 'a pair of doves or two young pigeons'.*

In the early days, this holy family is technically not altogether holy. Leviticus 12 is clear that when a woman has given birth to a boy, she is unclean for 40 days (80 days for a girl). So, for those 40 days, Mary was 'unclean' and could not enter the temple or touch anything sacred. These were known as the days of her purification and were brought to an end by the offering of two sacrifices—a lamb and a pigeon or dove. This was reduced to just two doves or pigeons if you were too poor to bring a lamb, so, it can be assumed, Mary and Joseph were poor.

Jesus' parents also have another religious duty—the ceremony of the redemption of the firstborn (Numbers 18:16). In those times, the first-born male child was regarded as belonging to God, so you had to 'buy' him back from God for the sum of five shekels. Mary and Joseph were diligent in observing the Law, although they might well have thought that they were 'above' such duties. After all, it was God that Mary carried in her womb, so how could she be unclean? How could they 'buy back' their son when really he belonged to God? If they did have such notions, though, they let them go because what they wanted to do more than anything else was to follow God in obedience.

Holiness is often found in humility. It is easy to think we are above doing certain things, but, while God never wants us to be anyone's doormat, the path to holiness is often found in those moments when our humanity chooses to be servant-hearted.

## Reflection

*How can you be the servant of the Lord today?*

MICHAEL MITTON

# The family welcomes foreigners

After [the Magi] had heard the king, they went on their way, and the star they had seen when it rose went ahead of them until it stopped over the place where the child was. When they saw the star, they were overjoyed. On coming to the house, they saw the child with his mother Mary, and they bowed down and worshipped him. Then they opened their treasures and presented him with gifts of gold, frankincense and myrrh. And having been warned in a dream not to go back to Herod, they returned to their country by another route.

By any reckoning the story of the magi visiting the family is a strange one. For a start, they came from a very long way away and followed a totally different religion. They were Gentiles and, thus, unclean. According to the customs of first-century Judaism, they should not therefore have been entering the home of law-abiding Jews.

Even today, though, if they appeared, we might well be suspicious of these gentlemen. They get their bearings by means of astrology—and that rather fatalistic view of the world, governed as it is by the movement of the stars and planets, is seriously at odds with our view of a personal God directing our affairs. Indeed, in many parts of the church, the practice of astrology is regarded as spiritually dubious, if not even evil. It is therefore easy to wonder what Mary and Joseph thought they were doing, opening their doors to these unclean pagans.

The answer is they instinctively recognised that these men listened deeply to God, even though their starting point appeared to be thoroughly pagan. The magi, through their particular customs and traditions, caught sight of something momentous happening in the universe that was earthed in Joseph and Mary's little home.

Thus, the story in today's passage shows us what open hearts Mary and Joseph had: they made no judgments about the magi or anyone else, and were looking and listening out for anyone who was genuinely set on seeking Jesus. We might well have judged the magi as misguided, but clearly they were anything but.

### Reflection

*How do we discern genuine searching in the hearts of others?*

MICHAEL MITTON

# The family in exile

When they had gone, an angel of the Lord appeared to Joseph in a dream. 'Get up,' he said, 'take the child and his mother and escape to Egypt. Stay there until I tell you, for Herod is going to search for the child to kill him.' So he got up, took the child and his mother during the night and left for Egypt, where he stayed until the death of Herod. And so was fulfilled what the Lord had said through the prophet: 'Out of Egypt I called my son.'

If travelling from Nazareth to Bethlehem seemed a long journey, this one to Egypt would have seemed monumental. It is Joseph who gets the message, from another night-time angelic visitor. The message he has for Joseph would be enough to chill anyone's blood. Herod had a reputation for extreme cruelty, killing even members of his own family, including his wife. The thought of this violence and hatred being directed towards his tiny baby would have been profoundly disturbing. Here is humanity at its darkest and such darkness threatens the life of the holy child.

We know very little about the family's time in exile. There were colonies of Jews in Egypt, though, so it is likely that Mary and Joseph would have been made welcome there. Egypt was regarded as a land where sorcery and witchcraft flourished, however, so it was a spiritually dangerous place. At the same time (as Matthew points out by making a reference to Hosea 11:1), the flight to Egypt was full of significance, paralleling the story of the people of God who had to go down to Egypt before the great act of deliverance by Moses. No doubt this crossed the minds of Joseph and Mary as they passed mighty pyramids and ancient monuments.

For them, then, Egypt was not a place of bondage or danger but the place of God's protection. It can be hard and disturbing when God takes us to somewhere unfamiliar, but with the eyes of faith we can detect the signs of God's blessing and protection.

**Prayer**

*Lord, when I feel far from home, grant me the eyes
to see your hand of protection.*

MICHAEL MITTON

# The family at home

After Herod died, an angel of the Lord appeared in a dream to Joseph in Egypt and said, 'Get up, take the child and his mother and go to the land of Israel, for those who were trying to take the child's life are dead.' So he got up, took the child and his mother and went to the land of Israel... and he went and lived in a town called Nazareth.

Once again, Joseph has a night-time angelic visitation—this time giving the all-clear for them to return to Nazareth, which, according to Luke, is their home town (Luke 1:26). Nazareth was a strategic and important town that lay in a hollow in the hills in the south of Galilee. It happened to be on a major caravan route, so anyone living there would have seen traders from different countries passing through and, of course, the busy movement of Roman troops.

It is here in this busy town that the family settles and then spends about 30 years in obscurity until Jesus appears by the river Jordan to be baptised by John (Matthew 3:13). Apart from the temple incident in Luke 2:41–51, which gives us one childhood story, we simply know that Mary and Joseph's family grew and Jesus appeared to be a normal child (Matthew 13:54–56). We get a sense that God was in no hurry: his son's mission would start all in good time. There was no acceleration of Jesus' education so that he could get on with kingdom of God work, but these silent years were valuable all the same. Jesus dwelt in a normal human home, nurtured by loving parents who knew that their task was to provide the environment in which their son could flourish.

Jesus humbled himself to enter this world as a human being, and that humbling included dwelling in a home where he needed to be loved and nurtured just like the rest of us. It was the human warmth of that family as much as anything else which equipped him to preach and live his holy message.

## Prayer

*Holy Jesus, help me to build a home that witnesses to the values of the kingdom of God.*

MICHAEL MITTON

# Supporting Barnabas in Schools
# with a gift in your will

For many charities, income from legacies is crucial and represents a significant aspect of their funding each year. Legacies enable charities to plan ahead and often provide the funding to develop new projects. Legacies make a significant difference to the ability of charities to achieve their purpose. In just this way, a legacy to support BRF's ministry would make a huge difference.

Take our Barnabas in Schools ministry, for example. In our increasingly secular society, fewer and fewer children are growing up with any real knowledge or understanding of the Bible or the Christian faith. We're passionate about enabling children and their teachers in primary schools to explore Christianity creatively, and to learn both about and from the Bible, within RE and Collective Worship.

Our Barnabas RE Days, using storytelling, mime and drama, are in great demand. They explore big themes (Who am I? Whose world? Who is my neighbour? It's not fair!) along with the major Christian festivals. We also offer specialist In-Service Training (INSET) sessions for teachers, along with a wide range of publications and a website with information, articles and downloadable resources.

Since 2011 we have introduced a brand new theme for each new academic year, with a Barnabas RE Day, INSET session, classroom resource and support materials on the web. We've encouraged many schools to take a fresh look at the Bible; we've helped them explore, through the eyes of faith and belief, values linked to the Olympic and Paralympic Games in London; most recently we've enabled them to explore Christianity as a worldwide faith. Our new theme for 2013–2014 invites them to explore the Christian themes and imagery in C.S. Lewis's 'Chronicles of Narnia' series.

A legacy gift could help fund the development of future themes for Barnabas in Schools.

Throughout its history, BRF's ministry has been enabled thanks to the generosity of those who have shared its vision and supported its work both by giving during their lifetime and also through legacy gifts. We hope you may consider a legacy gift to help us continue to take this work forward in the decades to come.

If you would like more information about making a gift to BRF in your will or to discuss how a specific bequest could be used to develop our ministry, please email enquiries@brf.org.uk or phone 01865 319700.

This page is intentionally left blank.

# The BRF

## Magazine

# The Managing Editor writes...

The BRF Magazine in this issue focuses on spirituality, beginning with an account by BRF Trustee and author Ann Persson of her silent desert retreat. Ann writes of receiving welcome 'fresh perspectives' on life as a result of her week-long experience in a very unfamiliar environment. A desert retreat might not be practical for us all, but maybe a single Quiet Day could offer similar refreshment in our walk with God. Why not consider one in the coming year?

Our 'Recommended reading' summarises three new BRF books, all of which explore some dimension of spiritual life—contemplative prayer, 'new monasticism' based on ancient Celtic spirituality, and meditation on poetry and related reflections. The authors of all these books aim to encourage growth to maturity and a deeper connection with God, and a common thread running through all three is that growth often comes from daring to engage with new ideas and practices, allowing God to 'stretch [our] capacity to new dimensions'.

Also in this issue, Chris Hudson of the Barnabas Children's Ministry team describes an exciting new RE Day for schools, based on the Narnia Chronicles by C.S. Lewis, especially *The Lion, The Witch and the Wardrobe*. Chris believes that these books, though written more than 50 years ago, can offer 'a fresh perception of ancient truths' through the power of the imagination. Having read the Narnia Chronicles for the first time at the relatively late age of 18, I can say that they revolutionised my image of God, and many of us will have had similar experiences of being refreshed and inspired by Lewis's stories. We hope that an upcoming generation of children in schools will benefit enormously from this new Barnabas RE Day theme.

The purpose of spiritual practice, we might say, is transformation. A meeting with God, whether it comes through silent prayer, an exploration of ancient traditions or the reading of a joyful and exuberant children's book, will not leave us unchanged. At BRF we remain committed to resourcing your spiritual journey in as many ways as possible.

*Lisa Cherrett*

# Adventure into silence in the Sinai desert

*Ann Persson*

The Lord said, 'I will allure her into the desert and there I will speak tenderly to her' (Hosea 2:14). These are the words that I took with me into the South Sinai Desert for a week-long retreat with the title 'Adventure into Silence'. It was held in October 2012 and was arranged by Wind, Sand & Stars, a company that has great experience in arranging desert retreats. I found myself in a random group of 17 people. We were led by Sara Maitland, whose book *A Book of Silence* (Granta, 2008) had created a good deal of interest.

The Sinai Desert is a remote and beautiful area, one through which the children of Israel would have passed in the years of wandering in the desert. Our adventure began as we turned off the highway and drove across the sand for two hours, reaching the camp in darkness. Our two Bedouin cooks produced a delicious meal and then it was time to lay out our sleeping bags on the sand, at a distance from one another, and sleep under the myriad stars. The tail of Halley's comet provided a spectacular display of shooting stars and the Milky Way was clearer than I had ever seen it before.

In the early hours of the morning, the moon crept over the hill and lit up the sky, and we woke to the colours of sunrise, which turned the mountains of sandstone to pink and orange and gold. The cooks were up and busy making bread; kettles of tea and coffee were on the fire by the Bedouin tent, which was used as a gathering-place. We breakfasted and then took time to introduce ourselves to one another and say why we had come on the retreat.

The morning was spent 'window shopping', which meant a tour of the mountains that flanked the wadi, our expedition leader pointing out the various places where we could find shade for times of meditation each day. We made our choices and after lunch we went off to our chosen spots for our first time of quiet. It took me a while to settle down, unused to the heat and the flies, but gradually stillness came over me and with it a sense of God's presence.

Each day fell into a gentle rhythm of rising and greeting one another by the fire, mug of tea or coffee in hand; a silent breakfast followed by Sara's input and then off to our space for meditation until lunch, which was also taken in silence; back to our space, which was becoming 'home', for the afternoon. As the temperature dropped a little and the sun began to set, there were optional walks led by our Egyptian guide, Moussa. There were new vistas to gaze at, for nothing was rushed; we saw on the sandstone ancient etched carvings of camels, but also of horses and ostrich, which proved that there must have been more vegetation at one time to support such creatures. As the sun set, the scrubby bushes looked as if they had been set on fire, reminiscent of Moses' experience.

We returned to camp for yet another cuppa and, as darkness fell and more wood was put on the fire and the candles lit, we took time to share with one another what had been the features of our day, both the challenges and the delights. Dinner followed, after which we listened to Moussa, who would tell us stories of the Bedouin—their history and culture —and would also speak about the Coptic tradition and St Catherine's Monastery, which we would visit on the penultimate day. Head torches were switched on so that we could find the way to our places on the sand and in no time we were snug in our sleeping bags, awed yet again by the stars overhead and grateful for the experiences of the day.

I have always thought of quiet days and retreats as punctuation marks in the writing of life: they help to make sense of it. This retreat was not only a full stop for me but also a new paragraph as God gently brought issues to my attention. He did indeed speak tenderly and gave me fresh perspectives on myself and on life back at home, for which I was very grateful.

I left my desert experience with another verse in my mind. It is from Song of Songs 8:5: 'Who is this coming up from the desert leaning on her lover?' If Christ is the Lover and I am the beloved, then that is just how I wanted it to be. It was a huge experience and all good.

I was 75 years old when I went on retreat; I am a great believer in saying 'yes' to any opportunities and challenges that present themselves, especially in this later stage of life. This was one that I will always treasure.

*Ann Persson is the author of* The Circle of Love *(BRF, 2010) and* Time for Reflection *(BRF, 2011). BRF Quiet Days are an ideal way of redressing the balance in our busy lives. Held in peaceful locations around the country, each one is led by an experienced speaker and gives the chance to be silent, pray and draw closer to God. See www.quietspaces.org.uk for further details.*

# Wandering into Narnia

*Chris Hudson*

At what age did you encounter your first 'Narnia' book? As a 9-year-old, I was introduced to *The Last Battle*, when Miss Wray, our teacher, read it aloud to us, chapter by chapter, over a succession of Friday afternoons. It was an interesting choice for a bunch of impressionable juniors, and she shared it with a passion. I can still hear her voice rising and falling as she related the final conflict between Narnians and Calormenes, the cynical dwarves shooting the horses with their bows and arrows, the chants of 'The Dwarves are for the Dwarves!', the oppressive sense of darkness and the chilling descriptions of Tash.

Nowadays, many children first encounter the stories through TV and films but the original books (with illustrations by Pauline Baynes) still retain their magic, remaining firm favourites with children and adults, despite the best efforts of stern critics such as Philip Pullman. It's all to do with the quality of Lewis's storytelling. The world he describes has a history and geography and folklore recognisably similar to our own, but its people and talking beasts lead a life bursting with freshness and exuberant energy. In Narnia, even the air seems to smell sweeter. Surely it *ought* to exist, somewhere?

As a teenager, I discovered that there was a 'Christian' element to Narnia too, but that only enhanced what I already knew. To me, there was already something recognisably 'right' about the stories.

When he first started writing the series, C.S. Lewis didn't plan a series of simple allegories.

*Some people seem to think that I began by asking myself how I could say something about Christianity to children; then fixed on the fairy tale as an instrument; then collected information about child-psychology and decided what age group I'd write for; then drew up a list of basic Christian truths and hammered out 'allegories' to embody them. This is all pure moonshine... Everything began with images; a faun carrying an umbrella, a queen on a*

*sledge, a magnificent lion. At first there wasn't anything Christian about them; that element pushed itself in of its own accord.*
'SOMETIMES FAIRY STORIES MAY SAY BEST WHAT'S TO BE SAID' FROM *OF OTHER WORLDS: ESSAYS AND STORIES*

Narnia wasn't meant to be a sermon with illustrations. Instead, as the story grew, Lewis' own personal theology shaped his imagination.

*I did not say to myself, 'Let us represent Jesus as He really is in our world by a Lion in Narnia'. I said, 'Let us suppose that there were a land like Narnia and that the Son of God, as He became a Man in our world, became a Lion there, and then imagine what would have happened.' If you think about it, you will see that it is quite a different thing.*
LETTER TO WALTER HOOPER, 'LITERARY CRITICISM'

For Lewis, the writing process was less calculated and more dynamic, so that what emerged on paper became much more interesting as it took shape. In Narnia, the death and resurrection of Aslan obviously parallel those of Jesus in our own world, but many other scenes are not exact parallels—and they're all the better for it. Lewis actively plays with ideas, using his characters to explore a whole range of moral crises and other human experiences. Edmund gives in to the temptations of the White Witch and her Turkish Delight, Uncle Andrew deludes himself about his scientific abilities and Digory, when he is sent to pick an apple from a magic tree, has to choose between obedience to Aslan and compassion for his mother. The fantastic realm of Narnia becomes a place in which to test and probe human dilemmas and the consequences of choice.

Lewis throws in some other surprising elements. While a few Christians might snort at the inclusion of Father Christmas in *The Lion, the Witch and the Wardrobe*, I remember being profoundly moved when a Royal Shakespeare Company production of the story did this scene rather well. After distributing his gifts to the Pevensie children, Father Christmas delivered a rousing shout to them and the theatre audience: 'And remember, the Lion LIVES!' Lewis' classical education also populated Narnia with characters and creatures from Greek mythology, such as Bacchus the god of wine, and river and tree spirits—the naiads and dryads. Other scenes suggest a whiff of World War II and the Cold War. Chilling mentions of the White Witch's oppressive 'secret police' deliberately reference the policies of totalitarian governments. When Digory and Polly view the ruined city of Charn, there's more than a hint of the desolation wrought by Total War—or even the atomic bomb. Lewis's views on contemporary progressive education are also very much in evidence when schools are mentioned: he didn't think much of it!

At BRF this year, to mark the 50th anniversary of C.S. Lewis's death, we thought it would be interesting and useful to create a Barnabas RE Day based on selected scenes from the Narnia books, focusing especially on *The Lion, the Witch and the Wardrobe*. Many primary schools are now trying to develop a creative curriculum that doesn't just 'teach the subjects' but systematically draws out the links between different areas of knowledge. (Children often learn better that way.) Religious Education especially lends itself to this, since the 'world of faith and belief' ought to connect with every part of human experience if it's genuine. So we decided to create something that used the Narnia stories to link RE and Literacy. Many children are used to 'doing Easter' once a year in school, but our Barnabas RE Day aims to enhance understanding of the first Easter by drawing parallels with what happened at the Stone Table in Narnia. Another key scene (Edmund's betrayal of his family) illuminates a similar scene in Eden, involving a serpent and a piece of fruit on another special tree.

Why do this? Because we believe in the imaginative life of children, and that some truths about the Christian faith are best discovered through stories. That's how Jesus taught the crowds in his own time, using parables to plant the seeds of new ideas in the human memory as teaching illustrations, but also leaving them as unexplained mysteries to flourish and grow in the unexplored corners of the imagination. Many of C.S. Lewis's stories have that same effect: they can present an apparently stale idea in a startling new light, giving a fresh perception of ancient truths.

At the time of writing, the Barnabas Children's Ministry team is still working on the schools package. The result will be made available to schools for the new school year in September/October 2013, just after the publication of our excellent new resource, *Teaching Narnia*, which has been written by Olivia Warburton (Commissioning Editor for Barnabas in Schools) especially to mark the anniversary. There will also be new free support materials for teachers made available on the website, and possibly a training programme for teachers. Will schools be interested? We hope so. (Of course, it always helps our marketing to cover a topic that simultaneously includes references to Christmas and Easter!) So as you read this, think of us beavering away, and ask yourself, is this something that the teachers at my local primary school need to hear about?

*Chris Hudson is a member of the Barnabas children's ministry team, based in the north-east of England. To find out more about Barnabas in Schools, visit www.barnabasinschools.org.uk.*

# Recommended reading

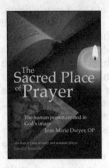

How confident are you about your faith? When Simon Reed moved to Ealing to lead an Anglican church, he found a group of people who were struggling and a church in danger of decline. Simon adapted the Celtic 'way of life' discipline for 21st-century use, helping his congregation discover a renewed spirituality. A rhythm of prayer is an essential part of that discipline—and prayer is a subject close to the heart of Jean Marie Dwyer, who regards people as being the 'sacred place of prayer'. We have a natural longing to bring God into our daily routine. So what can we expect when we encounter God in this way? Joy MacCormick's aim in *Moments of Grace* is to help you come to know God better, to help you move forward into a deeper connection, a richer relationship and an increasingly confident faith.

## The Sacred Place of Prayer
### The human person created in God's image
Jean Marie Dwyer, OP

Jean Marie Dwyer writes, 'I began this book from a desire to share with as many people as possible the great gift of prayer, to show that it is not a complicated set of methods or exercises, but as simple as living life, being ourselves and bringing God into our daily routine.'

There are many books available on the subject of prayer, so why add another one? The uniqueness of Jean Marie's approach is the conviction that prayer, even contemplative prayer, is natural to everyone because we are created for God and reflect God. As created humans, we are the sacred place of prayer.

What does that mean? In the first three chapters, she explores in a very accessible style the philosophical, biblical and theological groundwork for the understanding of the human person as the sacred place of prayer. She moves from this foundation to consider what it means to be a contemplative.

*The contemplative life does not divorce us from the world or from reality. True contemplative prayer emanating from our innermost centre does not separate us from the real needs of God's people; instead, we become the locus of God's saving action toward the world… The gift of the God-life and the work of grace are not alien to our human capacity but simply stretch that capacity to its true dimensions. Throughout the tradition, beginning with the scriptures, love of God and love of neighbour are inseparable. Union with God is impossible without a corresponding oneness with our neighbour (1 John 4:20).*

Within us all is a deep need for love and a place of belonging. Jean Marie's chapters on desert spirituality, illusions and finding our centre give insight into how we find our true self and our place of home and belonging:

*An inward stillness helps us to seek God in the daily ordinariness of our lives… Even a momentary pause in a busy day can be an oasis of stillness to re-centre ourselves. Equally important is stilling the unceasing chatter of our thoughts. In a society where noise and distractions are normal fare, such a commitment to silence takes courage. The early monastic tradition clearly understood and taught this truth. No moment, no situation, no pain or mis-understanding can separate us from God's presence, but each one calls us to search more deeply for the face of God.*

The book concludes by considering Mary the mother of Jesus.

*Mary is the sacred space in which the Word of God was conceived. In her openness to God's plan and her response to the Word, we have the model for our discipleship and an illustration for becoming the sacred space for God.*

Much of what is included in this book is drawn from years of reflective study, *lectio divina* and Jean Marie's own gradual formation through study and prayerful interaction with the scriptures in the Dominican community and in solitary prayer. The book includes practical exercises at the end of each chapter to 'earth' the lessons learned in the reader's own experience. An appendix provides a helpful guide to developing the practice of *lectio divina*.

*Perhaps, as you read these pages, you will discover that prayer is so much more than you thought. My hope is that this discovery may continue, deepen and be the beginning and end of all you do in life. Take time for wonder and awe at small things, at existence, at life, at the love we can share with one another. It opens the door to God.*

*ISBN 978 0 85746 241 1, pb, 128 pages, £6.99*

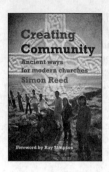

## Creating Community
### Ancient ways for modern churches
### Simon Reed

Based on the author's own years of exploration of Celtic spirituality through membership of the international Community of Aidan and Hilda, this book draws inspiration from a number of ancient spiritual practices. Simon explores how churches can base themselves around a Way of Life, a network of Soul Friends, and a Rhythm of Prayer, the building blocks of what many are now calling a 'new monastic' spirituality. The aim is to help Christians grow to maturity and create genuine community at a local level.

*ISBN 978 0 85746 009 7, pb, 144 pages, £7.99*

## Moments of Grace
### Reflections on meeting with God
### Joy MacCormick

'This book is, I hope, like a collection of keys to open awareness to the richness, diversity, wonder and mystery we name as "God". Meditative verse and related devotional pieces explore the delight, frustration, darkness and light of intimacy and abandonment in relationship with that God. I invite you to enter the sacred space of your own experience of the Holy and to move beyond familiarity into the unknown, daring to explore images and encounters that may be unfamiliar, even uncomfortable or challenging at times. In the course of that exploration, may you feel encouraged to step into a deeper relationship with God, with others and with your own self.' *(Joy MacCormick)*

*ISBN 978 0 85746 224 4, pb, 112 pages, £6.99*

To order copies of any of these books, please turn to the order form on page 155 or visit www.brfonline.org.uk.

# SUPPORTING BRF'S MINISTRY

As a Christian charity, BRF is involved in seven distinct yet complementary areas.

- **BRF** (www.brf.org.uk) resources adults for their spiritual journey through Bible reading notes, books and Quiet Days. BRF also provides the infrastructure that supports our other specialist ministries.
- **Foundations21** (www.foundations21.net) provides flexible and innovative ways for individuals and groups to explore their Christian faith and discipleship through a multimedia internet-based resource.
- **Messy Church** (www.messychurch.org.uk), led by Lucy Moore, enables churches all over the UK (and increasingly abroad) to reach children and adults beyond the fringes of the church.
- **Barnabas in Churches** (www.barnabasinchurches.org.uk) helps churches to support, resource and develop their children's ministry with the under-11s more effectively .
- **Barnabas in Schools** (www.barnabasinschools.org.uk) enables primary school children and teachers to explore Christianity creatively and bring the Bible alive within RE and Collective Worship.
- **Faith in Homes** (www.faithinhomes.org.uk) supports families to explore and live out the Christian faith at home.
- **Who Let The Dads Out** (www.wholetthedadsout.org) inspires churches to engage with dads and their pre-school children.

At the heart of BRF's ministry is a desire to equip adults and children for Christian living—helping them to read and understand the Bible, explore prayer and grow as disciples of Jesus. We need your help to make an impact on the local church, local schools and the wider community.

- You could support BRF's ministry with a one-off gift or regular donation (using the response form on page 153).
- You could consider making a bequest to BRF in your will.
- You could encourage your church to support BRF as part of your church's giving to home mission—perhaps focusing on a specific area of our ministry, or a particular member of our Barnabas team.
- Most important of all, you could support BRF with your prayers.

If you would like to discuss how a specific gift or bequest could be used in the development of our ministry, please phone 01865 319700 or email enquiries@brf.org.uk.

**Whatever you can do or give, we thank you for your support.**

# BIBLE READING RESOURCES PACK

Thank you for reading BRF Bible reading notes. BRF has been producing a variety of Bible reading notes for over 90 years, helping people all over the UK and the world connect with the Bible on a personal level every day.

Could you help us find other people who would enjoy our notes?

We produce a Bible Reading Resource Pack for church groups to use to encourage regular Bible reading.

**This FREE pack contains:**

- Samples of all BRF Bible reading notes.
- Our Resources for Personal Bible Reading catalogue, providing all you need to know about our Bible reading notes.
- A ready-to-use church magazine feature about BRF notes.
- Ready-made sermon and all-age service ideas to help your church into the Bible (ideal for Bible Sunday events).
- And much more!

**How to order your FREE pack:**

- Visit: www.biblereadingnotes.org.uk/request-a-bible-reading-resources-pack/
- Telephone: 01865 319700 between 9.15 and 17.30
- Post: Complete the form below and post to: Bible Reading Resource Pack, BRF, 15 The Chambers, Vineyard, Abingdon, OX14 3FE

Name _____

Address _____

_____

_____ Postcode _____

Telephone _____

Email _____

Please send me _____ Bible Reading Resources Pack(s)

This pack is produced free of charge for all UK addresses but, if you wish to offer a donation towards our costs, this would be appreciated. If you require a pack to be sent outside of the UK, please contact us for details of postage and packing charges. Tel: +44 1865 319700. Thank you.

BRF is a Registered Charity

ND0313

# BRF MINISTRY APPEAL RESPONSE FORM

I want to help BRF by funding some of its core ministries. Please use my gift for:
- ❏ Where most needed ❏ Barnabas Children's Ministry ❏ Foundations21
- ❏ Messy Church ❏ Who Let The Dads Out?

Please complete all relevant sections of this form and print clearly.

Title _____ First name/initials _____ Surname _____

Address _____

_____ Postcode _____

Telephone _____ Email _____

## Regular giving

If you would like to give by standing order, please contact Debra McKnight (tel: 01235 462305; email debra.mcknight@brf.org.uk; write to BRF address).

If you would like to give by direct debit, please tick the box below and fill in details:

❏ I would like to make a regular gift of £ _____ per month / quarter / year (delete as appropriate) by Direct Debit. (Please complete the form on page 159.)

## One-off donation

Please accept my special gift of
❏ £10 ❏ £50 ❏ £100 (other) £ _____ by

❏ Cheque / Charity Voucher payable to 'BRF'
❏ Visa / Mastercard / Charity Card
(delete as appropriate)

Name on card _____

Card no. ❏❏❏❏ ❏❏❏❏ ❏❏❏❏ ❏❏❏❏

Start date ❏❏ ❏❏     Expiry date ❏❏ ❏❏

Security code ❏❏❏

Signature _____ Date _____

❏ I would like to give a legacy to BRF. Please send me further information.

**If you would like to Gift Aid your donation, please fill in the form overleaf.**

**Please detach and send this completed form to:** Debra McKnight, BRF, 15 The Chambers, Vineyard, Abingdon OX14 3FE.   BRF is a Registered Charity (No.233280)

# GIFT AID DECLARATION

## Bible Reading Fellowship

Please treat as Gift Aid donations all qualifying gifts of money made

today ☐   in the past 4 years ☐   in the future ☐   (tick all that apply)

I confirm I have paid or will pay an amount of Income Tax and/or Capital Gains Tax for each tax year (6 April to 5 April) that is at least equal to the amount of tax that all the charities that I donate to will reclaim on my gifts for that tax year. I understand that other taxes such as VAT or Council Tax do not qualify. I understand the charity will reclaim 25p of tax on every £1 that I give on or after 6 April 2008.

### Donor's details

Title _____ First name or initials _____ Surname _____

Full home address _____

_____

Postcode _____

Date _____

Signature _____

Please notify Bible Reading Fellowship if you:
- want to cancel this declaration
- change your name or home address
- no longer pay sufficient tax on your income and/or capital gains.

If you pay Income Tax at the higher or additional rate and want to receive the additional tax relief due to you, you must include all your Gift Aid donations on your Self-Assessment tax return or ask HM Revenue and Customs to adjust your tax code.

# BRF PUBLICATIONS ORDER FORM

| Please send me the following book(s): | | Quantity | Price | Total |
|---|---|---|---|---|
| 241 1 | The Sacred Place of Prayer (*J.M. Dwyer*) | _____ | £6.99 | _____ |
| 009 7 | Creating Community (*S. Reed*) | _____ | £7.99 | _____ |
| 224 4 | Moments of Grace (*J. MacCormick*) | _____ | £6.99 | _____ |
| 161 2 | The Gingerbread Nativity (*R. Boyle*) | _____ | £6.99 | _____ |
| 265 7 | Real God in the Real World (*T.O. Hughes*) | _____ | £7.99 | _____ |
| 750 1 | The Circle of Love (*A. Persson*) | _____ | £5.99 | _____ |
| 876 8 | Time for Reflection (*A. Persson*) | _____ | £8.99 | _____ |
| 256 5 | Teaching Narnia (*O. Warburton*) | _____ | £6.99 | _____ |

Total cost of books £ _____

Donation £ _____

Postage and packing £ _____

TOTAL £ _____

| POSTAGE AND PACKING CHARGES | | | | |
|---|---|---|---|---|
| order value | UK | Europe | Surface | Air Mail |
| £7.00 & under | £1.25 | £3.00 | £3.50 | £5.50 |
| £7.01–£30.00 | £2.25 | £5.50 | £6.50 | £10.00 |
| Over £30.00 | free | prices on request | | |

Please complete the payment details below and send with payment to: **BRF, 15 The Chambers, Vineyard, Abingdon OX14 3FE**

Name _____

Address _____

_____ Postcode _____

Tel _____ Email _____

Total enclosed £ _____ (cheques should be made payable to 'BRF')

**Please charge my** Visa ❏ Mastercard ❏ Switch card ❏ with £ _____

Card no: ☐☐☐☐ ☐☐☐☐ ☐☐☐☐ ☐☐☐☐ ☐☐☐☐

Expires ☐☐☐☐ Security code ☐☐☐

Issue no (Switch only) ☐☐☐

Signature (essential if paying by credit/Switch) _____

## NEW DAYLIGHT INDIVIDUAL SUBSCRIPTIONS

❏ I would like to take out a subscription myself:

Your name _____

Your address _____

_____ Postcode _____

Tel _____ Email _____

Please send *New Daylight* beginning with the January 2014 / May 2014 /
September 2014 issue: (delete as applicable)

| (please tick box) | UK | SURFACE | AIR MAIL |
|---|---|---|---|
| NEW DAYLIGHT | ❏ £15.00 | ❏ £21.60 | ❏ £24.00 |
| NEW DAYLIGHT 3-year sub | ❏ £37.80 | | |
| NEW DAYLIGHT DELUXE | ❏ £18.99 | ❏ £29.10 | ❏ £31.50 |
| NEW DAYLIGHT daily email only | ❏ £12.00 (UK and overseas) | | |

Please complete the payment details below and send with appropriate
payment to: **BRF, 15 The Chambers, Vineyard, Abingdon OX14 3FE**

Total enclosed £ _____ (cheques should be made payable to 'BRF')

**Please charge my** Visa ❏ Mastercard ❏ Switch card ❏ with £ _____

Card no: [ ][ ][ ][ ][ ][ ][ ][ ][ ][ ][ ][ ][ ][ ][ ][ ][ ][ ]

Expires [ ][ ][ ][ ]   Security code [ ][ ][ ]

Issue no (Switch only) [ ][ ][ ][ ]

Signature (essential if paying by card) _____

To set up a direct debit, please also complete the form on page 159 and send
it to BRF with this form.

BRF is a Registered Charity

ND0313

## NEW DAYLIGHT GIFT SUBSCRIPTIONS

❏ I would like to give a gift subscription (please provide both names and addresses:

Your name _____

Your address _____

_____ Postcode _____

Tel _____ Email _____

Gift subscription name _____

Gift subscription address _____

_____ Postcode _____

Gift message (20 words max. or include your own gift card for the recipient)

_____

_____

Please send *New Daylight* beginning with the January 2014 / May 2014 / September 2014 issue: (delete as applicable)

| (please tick box) | UK | SURFACE | AIR MAIL |
|---|---|---|---|
| NEW DAYLIGHT | ❏ £15.00 | ❏ £21.60 | ❏ £24.00 |
| NEW DAYLIGHT 3-year sub | ❏ £37.80 | | |
| NEW DAYLIGHT DELUXE | ❏ £18.99 | ❏ £29.10 | ❏ £31.50 |
| NEW DAYLIGHT daily email only | ❏ £12.00 (UK and overseas) | | |

Please complete the payment details below and send with appropriate payment to: **BRF, 15 The Chambers, Vineyard, Abingdon OX14 3FE**

Total enclosed £ _____ (cheques should be made payable to 'BRF')

**Please charge my** Visa ❏ Mastercard ❏ Switch card ❏ with £ _____

Card no: ⬚⬚⬚⬚ ⬚⬚⬚⬚ ⬚⬚⬚⬚ ⬚⬚⬚⬚ ⬚⬚⬚⬚

Expires ⬚⬚⬚⬚ Security code ⬚⬚⬚

Issue no (Switch only) ⬚⬚⬚⬚

Signature (essential if paying by card) _____

To set up a direct debit, please also complete the form on page 159 and send it to BRF with this form.

# DIRECT DEBIT PAYMENTS

Now you can pay for your annual subscription to BRF notes using Direct Debit. You need only give your bank details once, and the payment is made automatically every year until you cancel it. If you would like to pay by Direct Debit, please use the form opposite, entering your BRF account number under 'Reference'.

You are fully covered by the Direct Debit Guarantee:

---

### The Direct Debit Guarantee

- This Guarantee is offered by all banks and building societies that accept instructions to pay Direct Debits.
- If there are any changes to the amount, date or frequency of your Direct Debit, The Bible Reading Fellowship will notify you 10 working days in advance of your account being debited or as otherwise agreed. If you request The Bible Reading Fellowship to collect a payment, confirmation of the amount and date will be given to you at the time of the request.
- If an error is made in the payment of your Direct Debit, by The Bible Reading Fellowship or your bank or building society, you are entitled to a full and immediate refund of the amount paid from your bank or building society.
  - – If you receive a refund you are not entitled to, you must pay it back when The Bible Reading Fellowship asks you to.
- You can cancel a Direct Debit at any time by simply contacting your bank or building society. Written confirmation may be required. Please also notify us.

---